THE ALCHEMIST'S HANDBOOK

(Manual for Practical Laboratory Alchemy)

Drei Novellen, 1932
The Alchemist's Handbook, 1960
  Second Edition, 1972
  Third Edition, 1981
  First Paper Edition, 1987
  Spanish Edition, 1980
  Italian Edition, 1980
  French Edition, 1980
From One to Ten, 1966
  German Edition, 1973
Praxis Spagyrica Philosophica, 1966
The Seven Rays of the QBL, 1968
  Revised and Expanded Edition, 1985
Praktiche Alchemie im Zwanzigstem Jahrhundert, 1970
Men and the Cycles of the Universe, 1970
  Spanish Edition, 1975
The Alchemist of the Rocky Mountains, 1976
  German Edition, 1980
Gently I Answered and Said, 1978
  German Edition, 1979

The Alchemist's Handbook

(Manual for Practical Laboratory Alchemy)

by

FRATER ALBERTUS

SAMUEL WEISER, INC.
York Beach, Maine

First published in 1960 by
The Paracelsus Research Society

This revised and expanded edition
first published in 1974 by
Samuel Weiser, Inc.
Box 612
York Beach, Maine 03910

First paper edition, 1987
Second printing, 1989

ISBN 0-87728-655-8
Library of Congress Catalog Number: 74-21127

Printed in the United States of America by
McNaughton & Gunn

CONTENTS

ILLUSTRATIONS

ORIGINAL OIL PAINTING AT PARACELSUS RESEARCH SOCIETY

*. . . out of the mists of doubt and despair emerge the twelve symbolic human types.
On their way to the temple of wisdom, to receive their initiation into the mysteries,
are they contemplating the new responsibilities awaiting them. It is the beginning of
a new phase of life eternal is The entry into the Sanctum Sanctorum Spiritii of the
Alchemists. . . .*

FOREWORD

This is the age of "how to do it" books. There is one on almost any subject you can think of. Since they fill a variety of needs, they have proven a boon. From them you can learn to paint, sew, plant a herb garden, build a brick barbecue in the backyard, become an interior decorator, and re-wire your own home. Almost every imaginable topic has been covered by these books. So if you assumed that this Manual falls in this category, you would be right—save for the simple fact that it is a great deal more.

Alchemy has exerted a strange fascination over mankind for centuries. The underlying philosophical theorem was that if the Divine Will had originally acted upon the *prima materia* to produce the precious metals and all else, why should not the alchemist—purified in mind and body, and an expert in the then known laboratory techniques—seek to emulate the same natural process in a shorter span of time? One has only to read a good history of chemistry, or to peruse a little of the vast alchemical literature, to become aware of its awful seductiveness. Men have left homes and families, squandered fortunes, incurred sickness and disease, gambled away prestige, social and other positions in quest of the goals perceived in the alchemical dream—longevity, perfect health, and the ability to transmute base metals into gold.

One must not be deluded by superficialities here. The alchemical adepts were patently dedicated and God-fearing men, holding the highest spiritual ideals conceivable. It is too bad more practitioners of the art did not perceive these goals.

Only recently, a journalist wrote that the Paracelsus Research Society which sponsors this Manual, offered to teach alchemy in two *weeks*. How could one be so myopic? Or illiterate?

In the early fourteenth century, Bonus of Ferrara spoke of Alchemy as "the key of all good things, the Art of Art, the Science of Sciences." Not only was the alchemist to be concerned with the purification of

6

metals and the elimination of sickness and disease from the human race, but he affirmed that Alchemy as Science and Art provided both a means to synthesize all the other sciences and a training of the intellectual and spiritual faculties.

The fascination that Alchemy has always held over mankind has surely been tainted in that rarely were there higher institutions of learning where promising students might study the ancient Art. Or where the proper techniques and methods might be learned as with other arts and sciences. No doubt, after the manner of the mysterious seventeenth century Rosicrucians, individual disciples were selected and trained by a master alchemist. We know that they had assistants and apprentices—for who would have kept the fires stoked in the furnaces, and washed the unending stream of glass and clay utensils employed in calcining, separating and distilling? Or who would have done all the thousand and one menial things that are so easily performed today that we barely have to think about them? But whether or not these assistants were ever encouraged to learn or to acquire the requisite disciplines and procedures—this is problematical.

In the vast literature on the subject, there is nothing that I have ever found that even pretended to demonstrate fundamental principles. Traditional alchemy, with its emphasis on piety, secrecy and allegory, is admittedly obscure. Over the years, I have met many men who could talk a good line about alchemy, but nothing practical ever emerged from them. Nor did anyone volunteer to demonstrate its basic truths in a laboratory or over the kitchen stove. Not one—until I met the author of this Manual some years ago. Not one—until I read the first limited edition of this Manual which literally is worth its weight in gold.

Incidentally, a few years ago I wrote something in recommendation of this manual, yet expressing criticism of its literary style, its form of expression, the innumerable typographical errors. This was silly and arrogant. For even if, theoretically, the book were written in the worst possible style, it would still be unique and a genuine masterpiece. Had it not been written and published, we would be the losers by far. It teaches with clarity, simplicity and accuracy the technical means whereby the lesser circulation may be accomplished. It should be a revelation to those who have not previously been introduced to this method of dealing with herbs. The Great Work is said to be essentially an extension of the same process, the same techniques, with the same universal philosophy. Many an alchemist of former years would have given his eyeteeth—or surely a small fortune—for this information. Many might have been spared disaster and destruction had they been familiar with the data contained in this Manual.

Descriptions of the alchemical processes are not readily understood in terms of modern chemistry. This is not to say that some formal training in high school or first-year college chemistry would not be useful. At the very least, it would have provided the dexterity to use the equipment also used in alchemy. But even if it were possible to translate the one system into the terminology of the other, the alchemists are haunted by the fear of revealing too much, too easily, or too soon—thus opening the way to abuse. Modern man has shown himself to be an adept in the art of abusing nature, as all our current emphasis on ecology and environmental pollution has indicated. So there is considerable justification for their doubts and for the allegorical mode of expression they have deliberately chosen.

But do not be deceived. Simply as this book is written, alchemy is a hard taskmaster. It demands patient and laborious service. There is no simple or easy path to the Great Work. It requires great dedication of purpose, sincerity and willingness to pursue this path to the bitter end—no matter at what cost.

One of the older alchemists stated that the fundamental process is so simple that even women and children could accomplish it. Maybe! It is only after one has arrived at the other shore, as it were, that one can realize that "except ye become as little children ye cannot enter the kingdom of heaven." Meanwhile, it requires effort, labor and prayer—or its equivalents—to achieve the simple child—like state capable of achieving the goals of alchemy. Not many have been blessed with the special genetic or psychological structure, or the perseverance, or the grace of God to find it.

But, if you really want to learn the basic principles of practical alchemy, here they are in this wonderful little Manual. There is no other book that I have ever encountered in all my long years in this movement that is one fraction as clear or as helpful. Forty years ago, I would have found it far more intriguing and illuminating than Mrs. Atwood's heavy and ponderous tome on which I exercised my wisdom teeth. Study it—and work at the processes described. Practice is so

much more rewarding and enlightening than a sterile "head-trip."
Ora et labore. Pry and work—but *work.* Without this you cannot even
begin. And this book describes *how* to go to work, and with what.

ISRAEL REGARDIE

PREFACE
To The First Edition

This little volume has been prepared under great difficulties, due to the immense scope of the subject matter and the consequent necessity of abbreviating so much valuable material. And yet it is almost impossible to condense this presentation of arcane knowledge without running the risk of causing greater confusion in the reader's mind.

For the neophyte on the path, Alchemy undoubtedly represents a great quest. To help ease somewhat the commencement of its study, the contents of this book—in the author's opinion—represent an aid in the form of an essential, yet simple, outline for the pursuance of practical laboratory Alchemy.

Whoever cannot comprehend what follows, has no alternative but to forget the whole matter for the time being.

I sense the rebuff awaiting me from students of the abstract sciences, and their accusation of empiricism, for presenting this work. However, this does not justify an apology on my part for what has been set forth in these pages. It represents an honest conviction based on practical experimentation in a university laboratory, as well as extensive tests and investigation in my private laboratory, originally founded on a firm belief in the truth to be discovered in the concealed teachings of the Alchemists—especially those of Paracelsus and Basilius Valentinus, and the authors of the *Collectanea Chemica*.

The ushering in of the Atomic Age should have made it comparatively easy to lay aside some of the prejudices which were previously held, yet they are still partially sustained by an incongruous criterion.

Why is it so unreasonable to assume—casting aside the overwhelming percentage of charlatans and imposters who called themselves Alchemists—that men such as Paracelsus and Valentinus did speak the truth about their discoveries? Is it because of what may seem an absurd terminology intermixed with metaphysical symbolism?

Suppose, then, that this represents one of the main arguments. A "Red Lion" or "Peacock's Tail" become, therefore, impossible childish nonsense, for the simple reason that, in current technical terminology, word combination such as "tetraphenylethylene dichloride"[1] are standard expression in the world of science. Similar letter and number combinations are no puzzle to one initiated into the marvels of chemistry. When such a term as "tetraphenylethylene dichloride" is expressed by means of its chemical symbols as:

$$2(C_6H_5)\ _2CCl_2 \text{ -2Zn-}(C_6H_5)2\ CCl \text{ - } CCl(C_6H_5)_2 \text{ - } 2HgCl.$$

this makes sense to the chemist. However, to the layman it represents only a meaningless scramble of letters and numbers. The chemical terminology, likewise, conveys no meaning to him.

Valentinus, who, with Paracelsus, shares fame as the Father of Modern Chemistry and Medicine, writes about himself: "Though I have a peculiar style in writing, which will seem strange unto many, causing strange thoughts and fancies in their brains, yet there is reason enough for me so doing; I say enough that I may remain by my own experience, not esteeming much of others prating, because it is concealed in by knowledge, seeing having alwaies the preheminence before hearing, and reason hath the praise before folly."

To the scientist, this may smack too much of empiricism and will be disparagingly discarded by him.

Is it really so unreasonable to accept the symbolism and word combinations of the Alchemists of the Middle Ages in the same light that we now take for granted the assertions of science?

The foregoing certainly deserves an honest answer.

In the following pages, should my hypotheses become evident to the reader, may they represent an attempt to keep the torch gleaming in these times of Stygian darkness. Centuries ago this flame was lighted by Alchemists whose names eventually will be honored by the children of those now making vain efforts to ridicule them.

It is anticipated that this handbook will not see an enormously large edition, since only a few may want to own a work on a subject which has fallen into such ill repute. Yet, those who have tried for some time

---

[1] One of the aromatic halogen derivatives.

to start experimentation in their laboratories in order to discover if there really is truth to be found in Alchemy, will find welcome and perhaps valuable help in its contents. There is no doubt in the author's mind that serious and prepared students can accomplish what is outlined in these pages.

Many years have elapsed since the writing of the present manuscript. After due deliberation, it has been considered timely now to hand it to the printer, so that others may benefit from it.

May it become what the title indicates, namely: a handbook for alchemystical novices.

With Peace profound,
FRATER ALBERTUS

Salt Lake City, Utah, U.S.A.
May 6, 1960

PREFACE

To The Second Revised Edition

It is with thanks that acknowledgment is given to Stanley Hurbert and Percy Robert Bremer, both Paracelsus Research Society students, for their efforts to revise the first edition of "The Alchemist's Handbook." Their help in this second edition is much appreciated since in its first appearance the book was full of typographical and grammatical error. The final proofs were read but the corrections not made before going to press. These errors have now been corrected.

It is to be hoped that by carefully following the instructions the practical results which may be obtained will prove of help to the serious student of Alchemy with visible manifestations in the laboratory. That such results are obtainable is beyond question as a great number of the students who have studied practical alchemy with the Paracelsus Research Society can testify. This applies not only to the Lesser Work with plants, but also to minerals and metals.

More than a decade of practical laboratory work taught openly with no cloak of secrecy or any oath of silence should be proof of the validity of this work.

FRATER ALBERTUS

CHAPTER I

INTRODUCTION TO ALCHEMY

What is Alchemy? This is the first and most vital question to be answered before a study of the following pages should be undertaken. This question can be answered to the satisfaction of the inquiring mind, but all careless paging through this book will be to no avail. If the reader has no previous knowledge of Alchemy and, moreover, no knowledge through conscientious study concerning mysticism, occultism, or related subjects, the answer to the above question will have little meaning. What, then, is Alchemy? It is "the raising of vibrations".

For this reason it is wise not to attempt to experiment with the laboratory outlines that follow. These experiments are only for those who have spent considerable time in spagyric research and who have proven to themselves that an honest endeavor has prevailed and that this same endeavor still motivates their true search for the highest Arcana, the lapis philosophorum. As all students of alchemystical literature have come to realize that the exact process for the opus magnum has never been completely revealed in simple language or put into print, they will appreciate the fact that here is given a detailed description of the lesser circulation.

In Alchemy there are the lesser and greater circulations. The former pertains to the herbal kingdom and the latter to the most coveted of them all, the mineral (metallic) realm. A correct understanding, and not just knowledge, of the herbal process will open the gate to the great Arcanum. Months and years of experimentation in your alchemical laboratory will prove the truth of this statement. The fact that Alchemy is a life's work will be accepted by those who have spent months and years behind books and retorts. It is this significant fact which provides our spagyric art with such an armor that no materialist can

14

pierce it. If it were not for the cleansing, purging, and aging of the alchemist-to-be over a great length of time, like the subjectum he is working with, how could it be kept from the profane and the unworthy? Only that which has stood the test of fire has been purified. That there is still a cloak of secrecy covering alchemical processes, and that this must yet remain so will have to be accepted by all aspiring alchemists. For personal greed has no place in Alchemy. The aim of all true Adepts is to help relieve a suffering mankind in its physical and spiritual misery. A nonacceptance of this excludes one automatically from the circle of Adepts.

My friends of the medical profession, as well as the pharmaceutical chemists, will readily disagree with me when reading what follows. This must be taken for granted and, in fact, has been so since what is presented here is so foreign to the standardized teachings in present day medical colleges. Since I agree with them, on their terms, it is only fair to ask that they think of the contents of this book in the terms of an alchemist. If this is impossible, then the book should be laid aside for the time being and forgotten until it can be examined by an open mind free from prejudice.

No attempt is being made here to write on allopathic therapeutics. This shall be left to those versed in this particular branch of healing. I am writing here about Alchemy because of the years of studies and experiments that have preceded this book, and because of the work that shall in all likelihood continue to follow. Since the scope of Alchemy is so immense, one earthly incarnation in many, if not most, cases is an insufficient time for the full completion of the work. In climbing the alchemist's ladder, there are many tribulations to consider involving time, money, heartaches—to mention only a few of the difficult steps. The aspirant then should think long and well before undertaking such an ordeal, for if he is not prepared all will prove unsuccessful.

The process in both the lesser and greater circulation is basically not expensive. In fact, it is relatively insignificant. But before this state can be reached much money, time, and effort can and, most likely, will be spent. It is for these reasons that an urgent appeal is made not to venture rashly into Alchemy, not to see oneself sitting in perfect personal health at the end of a rainbow with the world at one's feet and with full pots of glistening gold. These are only illusions and will prove to be but sensational and glamorous fata morgana; they will not satisfy the soul. There is more to be gained in Alchemy than vainglory. This, in fact, cannot be obtained in Alchemy. Such vainglory is as far from the true goals of Alchemy as night is from day. This brings us back to the simple statement made at the beginning of this chapter: "Alchemy is the raising of the vibrations." He who sees no meaning in this seemingly unimportant sentence has no right to attempt alchemical experimentation. Such a person is like one who claims that since he knows all the letters of the alphabet he can, therefore, read any language as they are all composed of letters from the same alphabet. But does he read with understanding when the letters are interchanged, forming words in different languages?   A chemist may know all the formulas and all the abbreviations of chemical terminology, but does he also understand what they really are? Their true origin? Their first state? This we shall leave for those who are concerned to answer. If all the foregoing statements do not discourage the aspirant and make him clap the book shut and put it away with disgust, perhaps then it will help him to find himself in this universe and to give peace and contentment to his soul. Hermetic philosophy, with its practical arcanum, repeats itself over and over again in the ancient axiom: "As above, so below. As below, so above."

It is questionable whether or not historical references to Alchemists of the past have a place in these pages. There have been so many books published already that have made it their business to elaborate on the history and romance of Alchemy. For this reason, no attempt is being made here to add to the wealth of biographical material supplied by such books. Our emphasis falls, rather, on present-day alchemystical experimentation, conducted in accordance with age-old practices. Our aim in these pages is to attempt to demonstrate and to reveal the truth of Alchemy in contemporary language, while still remaining in harmony with ancient rules and rituals, according to the Alchemist's Oath. The practice of Alchemy, not only in earlier times but in our own day as well, should be undertaken only with the greatest solemnity. This can best be illustrated by the following oath from *Theatrum Chemicum Britannicum* (London, 1652). This oath, in only slightly modified form, is still being used by present day Adepts:

"Will you with me tomorrow be content,
Faithfully to receive the blessed Sacrament,
Upon this Oath that I shall heere you give,
For ne Gold ne Silver as long as you live,
Neither for love you beare towards your Kinne,
Nor yet to no great Man preferment to wynne:
That you disclose the secret that I shall you teach,
Neither by writing nor by no swift speech;
But only to him which you be sure
Hath ever searched after the seacrets of Nature?
To him you may reveale the seacrets of this Art,
Under the Covering of Philosophie before this world yee depart."

Sooner or later, most students experience a desire to find an Adept in order to become his pupil or disciple. But no matter how sincere such a desire is, it is futile for the student to attempt to locate a teacher versed in the Grand Arcanum. "When the pupil is ready, the Master will appear." This ancient precept still holds true. One may search, one may aspire, one may work and study hard until the wee hours of the morning, and yet it will not be evidence that he or she will ever attain that priceless jewel: the Grand Arcanum. For it takes more than mere study. An honest heart, a clean heart, a true heart, a benevolent and contrite heart accomplishes more than all the book learning can ever do. Yet, strangely enough, learning must accompany the virtues just cited. Without a knowledge and an understanding of natural laws and their corresponding spiritual parallels, no one could ever truly be called an Alchemist or a Sage.

I am not attempting to vindicate Alchemy. It needs no vindication. I am advocating the truth in Alchemy, for it is a most wonderful experience to have come to a realization. To experience! To realize! To have found "the light that shined in the darkness."

All the foregoing may seem so discouraging. Perhaps a heavy doubt may weigh upon the heart of the lover of Alchemystical Research. Whatever the cause or whatever its effects may be, a tremendous responsibility is connected with it. He who has read about the lives of the Alchemists has found that most often many years had to elapse before their goal was reached. Not everyone was as fortunate as Eirenaeus Philalethes who writes that in his 23rd year that great blessing in the form of the *lapis philosophorum* was attained. Many had to await another incarnation before they proved themselves worthy and ready to receive it. But, if all doubts are put aside and if a firm Belief has grown into a strong Faith, then that quickening moment that produces knowledge will eventually help one to come to "Understand," to "Realize" the oneness of the universe, the secret behind Creation and the unfolding of cosmic consciousness.

This brings us to the natural questions: "What is the secret of creation? And what constitutes life force?" These questions must be answered before the would-be Alchemist can accomplish anything in his laboratory.

Since everything that grows comes from a seed, the fruit must be contained in its seed. Mark this well, for here lies the secret of creation. The raising of specimen, as said before, is the raising of vibrations. Herbs, animals, as well as minerals and metals, grow from seed. To understand this secret of nature, which is only partly revealed to mankind generally, constitutes the main theoretical subject in Alchemy. Once this is known, then only the proper understanding is necessary in order to obtain results in the raising or elevating of specimen, which is nothing else but transmutation. If we can help nature in her ultimate goal, that of bringing her products to perfection, then we are in harmony with her laws. Nature does not resent an artificial effort, or a shortcut, to bring about perfection. To illustrate: the seed of a tomato may be put into the ground late in the fall. Snow and ice may cover it during the winter. But no tomato plant will grow during this time, outdoors in freezing temperatures. However, if the same seed is planted inside where sufficient warmth and moisture is provided, and if it is placed in the proper matrix it will grow into a plant and bear fruit. This is not contrary to nature. It is in harmony with the natural laws. For fire (heat), water, air, and earth are all that are necessary to cause a seed to grow and bear its predestined fruit. The life force originates not in fire, earth, air, and water. This life force is a separate essence which fills the universe. This essence, or fifth essence (quintessence), is the truly important object that alchemists seek. It is the fifth of the four: fire, water, air, and earth, and is the most important one for the alchemist to find and then to separate. After such a separation has taken place, the answer to what lies behind the secret of creation will then manifest itself partly in the form of a dense smoke-like vapor that settles, after passing through the condenser tube, into a water-like substance of a yellowish color carrying with itself something oily which gives the tinge to the extracted water. This oily substance, or alchemical Sulphur, is just as essential to alchemical preparations as Salt and Essence. I do not wish to go into this any further at this point, as this will be treated more explicitly later on.

A repetition of certain phrases and sentences may be found throughout this book. This is not arbitrary; they have been purposely inserted in order to emphasize certain important points more strongly. Much that is written here must be reread many a time in order to lift the veil. This only can be accomplished individually by each student. That which follows will be discovered when the practical experimentation takes place in the laboratory.

Now to the alchemist's laboratory. This usually takes on a sinister coloring as one's imagination runs wild. Even today, so-called religious people are inclined to discuss Alchemy in rather subdued whispers because, so they claim, it is the devil's work. Ignorance is bliss to some, and no one has a right to take another out of his or her bliss. We must ignore those that have religious scruples against Alchemy, as we do not intend to convert anybody. The aim laid down here is to help the alchemical aspirant on his laborious road. This road begins in the laboratory. Everything in the laboratory revolves around the fire or its emanation: heat. The rest is composed of a few flasks, a condenser, and some ingenuity. It sounds rather simple and really is so. What about all the other instruments that clutter up an alchemist's laboratory, as pictures would have us believe? Just as an artist needs only canvas, paint, and brushes to paint a picture, but may add an indefinite number of other related objects to his studio, so may an alchemist add other related equipment as he sees fit. No doubt he is going to experiment and probe deeper into the mysteries to unlock one after another. Once the soul hungers and thirsts for truth and the unfoldment of nature's laws, there is no end to its search until the ultimate has been reached.

Where should a laboratory be located? How can one practice Alchemy in a crowded city? Such questions will have to be answered individually by each student. A corner in an attic or a place in the basement is sufficient, as long as there is a continuous source of heat available. He who wishes to practice our spagyric work will have to do all the work himself. How fortunate! How else could it be? How else can one appreciate the experience if he does not arrive at the crucial point of knowledge by his own individual efforts? Enough has been said now concerning the hardships and disappointments that undoubtedly will be encountered. If the student, in spite of these difficulties, still wishes to enter the portals of the spagyrist's holy temple, he will find a welcome guide in the following pages. These unfold, in simple language, the process of the lesser circulation.

Those who wait for a complete description, in similar language, of the Grand Arcanum will wait in vain. It cannot be given. It is not permissible. But—and this is of utmost significance—he who can accomplish in his laboratory what the following pages present by way of instruction, can surely accomplish the Grand Arcanum, *if he is ready*. The preparation may take years or even tens of years. No time limit can be set. Some have a natural or inherited tendency, or gift, to delve into the mysteries. Some can never even enter. The "why" for this has no place here. But to those who are ready to travel the royal road of Alchemy, I say, "Patience! Patience! Patience! Think and live cleanly and charitably and dwell always in truth—that which *you* honestly consider and believe to be the truth." Such a neophyte cannot fail then. Remember, "Seek and ye shall find; knock, and it shall be opened unto you."

The wisdom of the Sages represents a culmination of all that is essential for men to have faith in, knowledge of, and understanding about. He who has attained such a state of illumination is indeed in harmony with the universe and at peace with the world. To reach this goal of enlightenment, the struggle in this mundane shell need not be of a violent nature, as some want us to believe; rather it should be a constant alertness to the possibilities that confront us in our daily lives, to raise our thought world above the drudgery of this everyday life, and eventually to find the peace within us. If one has not undergone the Alchemy of the inner self, or transcendental Alchemy, as it has been termed, he will find it extremely difficult to obtain results in his practical laboratory experimentation. He may produce things he knows nothing about, consequently passing them up as worthless. It is not sufficient only to know; it is understanding that crowns our work. It is here the wisdom of the Sages and Adepts helps to bring about an understanding within the individual concerning that which he knows but does not understand.

In Alchemy there is only one way that leads to results. The aspirant must show his worthiness and his sufficient preparation. This preparation extends over many and varied subjects, but most of all does it concern the search for truth. The living, waking, or conscious state must be immersed in the truthfulness that speaks out of every word and action. There must be a love for mankind that knows no passion, a readiness to gladly share one's entrusted material possessions with others, and a willingness to put the needs of mankind above personal desires. All of these virtues one must acquire first. Only then will the wisdom of the Sages and Adepts begin to make sense. Then Nature will become a willing companion to serve us. The world, as we will then realize it, begins to take on form and shape, whereas previously it enshrouded us in a haze which our vision could not penetrate. We will come to know God. Illumination will enlighten our whole life. It will cease to be a mere fight for an existence, for the Divine will have entered our hearts. Peace profound will dwell within and surround us amidst turmoil and strife. This the wisdom of the Sages will help us to attain. But only our own preparation and proper living will let us obtain it. We must do the work ourselves, for no one can do it for us. We will begin to realize that everything is no longer so individualistic as it seemed before. *We* is the term in which we will think. *We*, God and I, humanity and I become entwined. The "I" loses its meaning; it becomes submerged in the Cosmic All. "I" becomes many, as part of many that has its ultimate in one. Individuality, though still existing, becomes "All-individuality." Hence we begin to realize that the "I" is only a segment of the Divine, an entity in itself but not the true self, that which is All, the Divine. The wise men, Sages, Adepts or whatever names we may give them, those who have become illuminated, meet on the same plane. They have climbed to the mountain top. Theirs is the mastership over the world below. They can see what happens below and that which will happen because of their far-reaching sight. Those in the valley, twisting and turning and searching behind obstacles are too close to the pattern of events to see it. Sages read Nature as an open book printed in clear type whose sentences they fully understand.

The writings left us by the Sages are typical for the correspondence of their thoughts and explanations. All agree with one another. Only the uninitiated believes he detects inconsistencies and seeming contradictions, due to a lack of understanding. Exemplary in its precision and profundity are the seven points dealing with Rosicrucian concepts as given during an extra curricular lecture to students of The Rose Croix University by the late eminent Sovereign Grand Master of that Order, Thor Kiimaletho*. The following is quoted from his lecture, "The Basic Rosicrucian Concepts":

"1. The Origin of the Universe is Divine. The Universe is a manifestation of, and an emanation from, the One Absolute Cosmic Being. All manifestations of life are centers of consciousness and expressions of the One Life within the framework of its material limitations. There is but One Life in the Universe—the Universal Life. It saturates and fills all forms, shapes, and manifestations of life.

"2. The soul is a spark of the divine consciousness in the Universe. As a drop of water is a part of the ocean and all water, so is the soul manifesting in material expression, a part of the One Soul in the Universe. In the human being it develops the personality and the individual expression.

"3. The soul-force possesses potentially the powers of the divine principle at work in the universe. The function of life on earth is to afford the opportunity of developing these potentialities in the personality. Since one incarnation on earth cannot possibly be sufficient, the personality must return again and again in order to achieve the maximum development.

"4. The moral law is one of the basic laws of the universe. It is likewise called the principle of Karma, the result of cause and effect, or action and reaction. There is nothing vindictive about this principle. It works impersonally like any law of nature. As the fruit is contained in the seed, so the consequences are inherent in the act. This principle guides the destinies of both men and nations. Knowledge of this principle gives man the power to control his own destiny.

"5. Life has a purpose. Life is not meaningless. Happiness is a very real thing and is a by-product of knowledge, action, and living.

---

* Thor Kiimaletho granted the author permission to quote from "The Basic Rosicrucian Concepts."

"6. Man has free choice. He has tremendous powers of both good and evil, depending upon his conscious realizations.

"7. Since the individual soul is part of the universal soul, man has access to powers he does not know, but which time and knowledge and experience will gradually reveal to him."

Hermetic philosophers have taught the very same fundamentals even as philosophers of the future will do, for that which constitutes truth will remain truth. It cannot be changed. But the theories of men and their opinions, which are incorrectly given by some as truth, are subject to change. Because one calls himself a philosopher does not necessarily make him such. Only he is a philosopher who has a sincere love for the wisdom that manifests universally and who strives as sincerely to apply it in his daily life. Wisdom is acquired through righteous living. It is understanding applied. The acquisition of a degree of Doctor of Philosophy, as conferred upon graduates in institutions of higher learning, does not make one a philosopher, as much as those in possession of such a degree may believe in their right to such a title.

To be acquainted with the history of philosophy, the lives and teachings of those called philosophers, is only a study and knowledge of their universal concepts and what has been derived from them. To be a philosopher, therefore, means to understand and live according to that understanding, knowing well that only by giving unhesitatingly and unselfishly will our belief in mankind be justified. When this has been realized, then only will Alchemy become something real. Transmutation always takes place on a higher plane, and in the physical world laws cannot be adhered to or violated without producing karmic manifestations. Beneficial karma, if it is permissible to use a term, because karma is impartial, is brought about by harmonious applications of natural laws. These natural laws must be adhered to if, according to predestined results, we wish to obtain what nature has decreed.

If the foregoing even in its very condensed form has made any sense at all to the student of Alchemy, it must be apparent then why that alchemical gem, which all alchemists desire to produce, has been called the *Philosopher's Stone*. How often it is that we use words and attach no meaning to them, only because we fail to understand.

CHAPTER II

THE LESSER CIRCULATION

It is difficult to understand alchemical terminology. The novice without proper mental and spiritual preparation usually interprets spagyric symbols in his or her own way, thereby starting on a laborious road of misconception that only years of painful experience can remedy. It is safe to say, and experience has taught it to be so, that all beginners in Alchemy have their minds set on obtaining the Philosopher's Stone. However justified this goal may be, nevertheless, without proper preparation, it is usually soon abandoned when after a comparatively short time of experimentation no results become manifest. Then Alchemy is condemned, called a fraud, or given similar names and erstwhile serious students, due to lack of proper preparation, disparage the true value of that which they do not understand.

In this chapter of practical alchemystical laboratory experimentation, the beginner will be *patiently instructed* on how to obtain the true alchemical herbal tinctures, extracts, and salts. As the reader will notice, "patiently instructed" has been emphasized. It may be well to commence this instruction by confronting the Neophyte with the prime requisite in alchemystical laboratory practice, namely, PATIENCE. This word should be painted in large letters and then hung above the alchemist's Athanor[1]. It is incomprehensible that anyone can accomplish anything in laboratory alchemy without the utmost patience. Later, personal experience will let the beginner come to a full realization of this important statement. If, therefore, the Neophyte believes himself or herself sufficiently endowed with this virtue, I shall most gladly open the door to my laboratory and guide the earnest

---

[1] This word was used by Paracelsus to designate the oven in which the fire was kept burning.

student in his mind's eye through the various processes which are necessary to obtain the desired results.

To begin with, the selection of herbs for medicinal purposes must be known to the aspirant. This means a fair understanding of herbs and their uses.

How to Collect and Prepare Plants

The different parts of plants should be gathered when their peculiar juices are most abundant in them.

Barks

The barks of either trunk, branches, or roots should be peeled from young trees in autumn or early spring. After shaving off the outer portion of the bark, cut thinly and place in a good position in the shade to dry.

Roots

These should be dug after the leaves are dead in the fall at which time all the strength has gone down into the root. But better still, dig them in early spring before the sap rises.

Seeds and Flowers

Only after they are fully ripened and in full bloom should seeds and flowers, respectively, be gathered. Then they should be dried quickly in the shade.

Medicinal Plants

These should be taken while in blossom for best results, but can be gathered at any time before the frost comes. Dry quickly in the shade.

Leaves

Leaves should be collected while the plant is in flower. Dry quickly.

Fruits and Berries

These should be picked when fully ripe. Dry quickly.[2]

---

[2] The progressive student will learn later on at what planetary times herbs should be gathered.

One of the best methods for drying herbs is to spread them thinly on clean paper, preferably on the floor, over which a constant stream of fresh air can pass.

Herbs, or all vegetable medicines, should be kept in a dry and dark place. Tin cans are to be preferred to other containers for storing powders. Roots are best kept in covered boxes. Tinctures and extracts should be kept in dark glass bottles to protect them from the action of light.

Let us suppose then that the herb known as Balm, Lemonbalm, or Melissa (Melisa officinalis) has been selected. After the selection of the desired herb from which the true alchemical medicinal potencies shall be derived, we shall now consider the principle ways of obtaining an extract. They are as follows:

1. Maceration
   The fresh or dried herb is soaked in water and left standing in room temperature.
2. Circulation
   The fresh or dried herb is circulated (percolated). This is accomplished by having a condenser over the flask which lets the moisture condense and drip back into the bottom container. It then repeats this process which is also known as reflux.
3. Extraction
   The fresh or dried herb is put in a thimble and both are placed in a Soxhlet Extractor for extraction.

Either of the three procedures can be used to obtain an extract. Water, Alcohol or Ether may be used as extraction media (menstrum).

The above three ways are chiefly employed to obtain the extract or the tincture. A tincture derived from a distillation with water does not contain as much of the essential essence of the herb as the macerated herbal extract obtained by immersion in alcohol or ether. To obtain all possible essence, including the oily substance inherent in the herb, the latter method, that by extracting it in an extraction apparatus (Soxhlet or other), is preferable.[3]

---

[3] This will be dealt with in a later chapter.

After the extraction of the essence, the herb will remain as a dead residue from which the life has been taken in the form of the liquid essence in either one of the above described three methods. These feces, as they are called, or in alchemical language, "Caput Mortum," meaning dead head, are then taken and burned to ashes. This is accomplished by taking the residue and placing it in an earthenware or porcelain dish which is placed over the fire. The contents of the dish are burned to a blackness from which state they will gradually change to a light gray color. After these ashes have become light, they should be placed into a mortar and ground to a fine powder with a pestle.

It is here where the differences between allopathic, homeopathic, and biochemic medicinal procedures become evident. Allopathic therapeutics generally use tinctures or salts (alkaloids), while homeopathic and biochemic therapeutics use salts (minerals triturated). The triangle is a great help in explaining the necessity of a conjunction of both the essence and salt to obtain a true manifestation as occurs only in Alchemy. To illustrate:

MANIFESTATION
(Perfect Medicine)

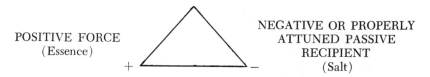

POSITIVE FORCE (Essence) +   NEGATIVE OR PROPERLY ATTUNED PASSIVE RECIPIENT (Salt)

If an herb, immersed or steeped in boiling water, produces a tea that helps to remedy bodily disorders, how much more effective must be the manifestations of an extract, or even conjunction of extract and salt, in the human body. It may be well for further demonstration to present here the three principal kingdoms of nature in their proper relationship, i.e., vegetable, animal, and mineral kingdoms. A common error that has been and is still being made is the intermixing of vegetable essence with animal or mineral salts. Since each constitutes a separate sphere or vibratory group, a mixture of these not properly attuned recipients will produce no manifestation. This is important, especially when producing the elixirs derived from the animal or even mineral kingdoms. It is because of a misunderstanding of these vital principles of Alchemy that such a furor has been caused among pseudo-alchemists when they have failed to produce any alchemical manifestations, while in their estimation these manifestations should have occurred. It is seemingly impossible to convey fundamental principles to newcomers in Alchemy without the use of analogy. Through concentration, from a commonly harmless substance, a poison can be produced. Therefore, it is also possible to produce from the same substance something which is equally non-poisonous.[4]

If the reader will follow patiently through the labyrinth of seeming contradiction, he will emerge truly triumphant at the end of its winding path; carefully avoiding prejudice and misconception, he will be able to see the light. To be sure, Alchemy is a slow process. It is evolution—the raising of vibrations. It is not a subject that can be mastered by means of the intellectual faculties alone.

The two principles of Essence and Salt have now been presented. However, before taking the next difficult step of joining the Essence to the Salt(and thus producing an alchemical manifestation), a few words dealing with what the Essence and Salt represent should be carefully noted by the reader.

(1) The Essence (Quintessence) or active force in the vegetable kingdom is the same in all plant life.

(2) The Salt or ashes to which any plant can be reduced differs from one plant to another.

This Essence, or "Mercury" as alchemists call it, is the life-giving energy that is manifest in all matter. The same Mercury exists throughout the animal kingdom, and the same Mercury throughout the mineral kingdom. Yet, and the reader will please note, although the Mercury is of the same origin, it is of a certain vibration in the vegetable kingdom, of a higher vibratory rate in the animal kingdom,

---

[4] Wisdom is a flower from which the bee its honey makes and the spider poison, each according to its own nature. (Author unknown)

and of a still higher rate in the mineral realm. It is for this reason that Mercury from the vegetable kingdom should not be mixed with the salts from either of the other two kingdoms. Each represents a separate unit. The animal eats herbs and contracts and cures ills from the same source. Where the cure fails, only the next higher ones will help. Even here it must be stated that the highest Elixir will not function indefinitely if the mind is not kept in proper condition. Humans, belonging to the animal group, eat both vegetables and meat. Therefore, they can be cured with both, i.e., vegetable essences in their first state, and more adequately with their own animal Salt and Essence (arcanum of blood). However, the most potent form of terrestrial manifestation is produced from the salts and essences from the minerals and metals. In its highest form (and brought to perfection only by man) this is known as the Philosopher's Stone. Nature in her performance does not produce the elixir of any of the three principalities. Each one, herbal, animal, and mineral elixir, can be produced only by art. Nature does not produce the Philosopher's Stone in the same sense that it forms the crystals of the earth.

From the foregoing it should have become clear to the reader that there are:

1. Three kingdoms or principalities as follows:
   a. Vegetable
   b. Animal
   c. Mineral

2. Each kingdom has its own Mercury. All three Mercuries are derived from the same original source, but manifest under different vibrations in each realm.

3. The Salt of each vegetable manifestation differs from one plant to another. This also holds true of all Salts from animal and mineral products.

4. Substances (Essence and Salt) should not be intermixed when elixirs or alchemical medications are prepared.

5. Alchemical elixirs are not products of natural formation, but of artificial production.

A further analogical illustration will perhaps clarify one common misconception—why the human being, belonging to the animal kingdom, does not stand above the mineral. The reader will bear in mind that we are dealing here with the physical aspects of Alchemy. To explain why human beings are endowed with reasoning powers that are not manifest in vegetables, minerals, and metals would bring us into transcendantal Alchemy. Here we are dealing with the physical phenomena.

If, by divine wisdom, man, as highest specimen of the animal realm, has been placed in the middle of the three kingdoms, it has been of necessity, since nothing in nature is based on chance. Man is holding the balance of the three kingdoms and can partake of any one according to his liking, having an alchemical laboratory in his own body to transmute inorganic matter into organic, and organic into spiritual matter.[5] Since these are actualities with which we are confronted, we must deal with them and attempt to understand them. Only laws that are basic and of true cosmic value enter Alchemy. There can be no speculation in Alchemy. Alchemy is based upon facts and, with patience, experimentation, and perseverance, the sincere student will obtain these facts. There is no other way than the one all Alchemists have traveled, and this is the way of experience.

All fundamental principles are the same throughout Alchemy. They apply to all three kingdoms. In mentioning the number three, it can now be stated that this number of manifestation will be found repeatedly in Alchemy. When in the foregoing only two substances, Mercury and Salt, have been mentioned, it was done purposely in order not to confuse the beginner. As there are three principalities or kingdoms, there are also three substances with which an Alchemist is continuously working. Without them nothing can be accomplished in Alchemy. They are Mercury, Salt, and Sulphur. They are represented by the following symbols:

---

[5] The human body contains some inorganic minerals in minute quantities from which it receives nourishment of a highly vibratory nature.

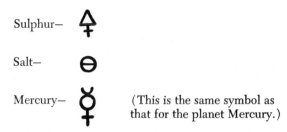

Sulphur—

Salt—

Mercury—   (This is the same symbol as that for the planet Mercury.)

As previously explained, alchemical Mercury is not the same as common quicksilver. Neither is Sulphur common sulphur or brimstone. Nor is Salt common table salt or sodium chloride.

Sulphur, that is, the alchemical Sulphur, is usually found in its oily form adhering to the Mercury. It must be separated by means of distillation. This yellow substance is the Sulphur that common alcohol extraction did not set free sufficiently. (With metallic Sulphur the difference will become even more noticeable.)

In the herbal process, the separation of the Sulphur from the Mercury (Essence) is not as essential as in the mineral work. Therefore, the beginner will not use the three alchemical substances separately, but will use Mercury and Sulphur combined and Salt separately. The first two (forming one liquid in the herbal extraction) are joined to the Salt, and from this combination, the alchemical medicine or elixir is then produced. In this way, from any herb an elixir can be made by art that is more potent than either the tincture, extract, or Salt taken alone, as is commonly prescribed by present-day therapeutics.

The foregoing is an attempt to present a synopsis of the fundamentals in Alchemy, the basic theory underlying all alchemical work. What follows is an example of the practice, in this case, a presentation of the procedure for obtaining alchemical elixirs from herbs. The process used in the herbal work differs only slightly from that employed with animal and mineral substances. One of the differences is the non-separation of the Sulphur from the Mercury in the herbal process.

In the instructions that follow, it is presumed that the spagyric novice already possesses a clear knowledge of what herbs are and what medicinal properties they contain. Only students equipped with this knowledge should proceed to the practical laboratory work described in the following pages.

CHAPTER III

THE HERBAL ELIXIR

In preparing the herbal elixir, we will use those parts of herbs that contain medicinal value. This may be the leaves, stems, roots, or flowers, depending upon the particular herb being used. This presupposes, of course, some understanding on the part of the students of the healing properties of herbs. Fresh herbs firstly should be dried in a warm place where there is an adequate circulation of air. If fresh, undried herbs are used in our work, it will be found that they contain much water which is of no value to us. When an herb is dried, the essence and sulphur remain in it and can be easily extracted. The water contained in fresh herbs will mix with alcohol and will only serve to increase the bulk. Therefore, the student should observe the following procedure:

1.—A sufficient amount of alcohol[1] should be rectified.[2]

2.—The herb selected for use should be finely ground in a mortar with a pestle.

3—The ground herb[3] is now to be placed in the thimble of an extraction apparatus. To this apparatus attach a flask half filled with the rectified alcohol. Now the fire should be lit under the flask in order to commence the extraction.

---

[1] Alcohol is derived from various sources. It is obtained from sugar cane, grain, corn, potatoes, grapes, wood, to name its most common sources. Therefore, all alcohol is not the same. This is especially significant where Alchemy is concerned. When we refer to the grain spirits we speak of that which is the essence of the grain. Thus it should be seen that alcohol is, therefore, the spirit or essence which is freed from the various sources from which we obtain it. Alcohol derived from wood is known as methanol and is poisonous if taken internally. The alcohol, or spirit of wine, obtained from wine is the best and most ripened essence of the vegetable kingdom. It has been claimed to have the highest vibratory rate of any essence in the vegetable kingdom and is, therefore, used as a menstrum to make extractions from herbs.

[2] To rectify alcohol, proceed as follows: Take any pure non-poisonous alcohol

A Soxhlet extraction apparatus consists of three parts:

1. Flask

2. Extractor and thimble

3. Condenser

The flask is at the bottom. The middle section is the extractor, which contains the thimble (a filter paper cylinder in which we have placed the herb to be worked upon). The condenser is the top section, which rests on the extractor. This is illustrated in the drawing on page 34.

4. After three or four extractions have made, it will be noticed that there is a definite change of color in the contents of the flask. Should a dark rim form on the flask, it will be necessary to lower

---

(190 proof spirits) and distill at 78 degrees C. Whatever is distilled at a temperature above 78 degrees C. cannot be used. Take all that has been distilled at not above 78 degrees C. and place this again in a clean flask. Re-distill at 76 degrees C. The distillate should then be distilled again. This is to be performed seven times from the first distillation. That which remains behind will become darker after each distillation. Finally, at the last distillation the distillate will be a crystal clear alcohol. (Do not use methanol.)

There is another method by which alcohol may be rectified. Distill again non-poisonous 190 proof alcohol at 78 degrees C. To every 1000 ml. of this distilled alcohol add 25 grams of potassium carbonate anhydrous. Let this stand for 48 hours. Shake occasionally. Distill the alcohol once again at 76 degrees C. The distillate will be a rectified alcohol.

The first method above is the old way to rectify. The second method is used today in modern chemistry. Experience will teach which method the individual alchemist will choose.

[3] Our rectified alcohol which is sufficient for herbal extractions must yet undergo another preparation before it is fit for mineral extractions. The rectified spirits of wine of the sages differs from the one described here for the herbal extraction.

It should also be mentioned that in preparing the rectified spirits of wine, it is preferable to use a red wine, the older the better. The wine should be a pure unfortified wine. Any wine that contains more than 17% alcohol by volume may be fortified with alcohol derived from sources other than grapes. When such is the case and wine thus altered is distilled, the distillate, therefore, will not be pure spirits of wine. For this reason the spirits of wine should be obtained only from wine containing less than 17% alcohol by volume, or else obtained from grape brandy. This is of great importance in Alchemy.

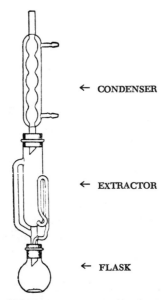

← CONDENSER

← EXTRACTOR

← FLASK

(This apparatus can be obtained from any chemical supply house
at a reasonable price.)

the fire, otherwise the Sulphur (oil) will be scorched and lose
its efficacy. It is preferable to use a water bath rather than an
open flame, as the water bath will prevent the scorching or burning of the delicate oil (Sulphur) contained in the extract (Essence).

5. When the alcohol coming through the syphon tube eventually
becomes clear, that is an indication that the extraction has been
completed. The thimble should now be removed and its contents
placed in an earthenware or porcelain dish. Place a wire screen
over the dish and light this residue which will ignite at once, due
to its being saturated with alcohol. Care should be taken that
there are no other flammable substances close by. This material
should be calcined to black ash. Grind this and then calcine again
to a light gray.[1]

---

[1] A prolonged calcination can change the gray to a reddish color which of
course is preferable, but this will require a long time.

6. The calcined ashes (Salt) are now placed into the lower flask. A sufficient amount of the extract is poured over this Salt. The flask is reattached to the extraction apparatus and circulation is started. This is to be continued until the Salt has absorbed the Essence and Sulphur. The extract in the lower flask should become lighter. When there is no further change in color, the Salt has absorbed all that is possible. If the extract becomes clear, pour it out of the flask and add more of the Essence until the Salt does not absorb any more.

7. Detach the flask and remove its contents. This is now the alchemical elixir in its first state. When warm it becomes an oily substance and will run. When cold it becomes solid again.

8. The potency of this elixir may be increased by calcining it in a calcining dish. This is then returned to the flask of the extraction apparatus, and the circulation is repeated with more of the extracted essence. Each time this is done, the potency will be increased.

The process can be carried a step further by placing the three combined substances in a glass flask which is tightly sealed and subjecting it to moderate heat for digestion. In this way a "stone" in the vegetable kingdom can be produced. (This must not be confused with the Philosopher's Stone.) While it is not absolutely necessary to produce a vegetable stone, it will nevertheless be of great help for further alchemical investigations, especially if one is not familiar with what a sublimate substance looks like. The potency of such a "stone" is far greater than any medicament in the form of an elixir, as described previously. This herbal "stone" will attract the Essence, Sulphur, and Salt of other herbs by immersion only. However, this is not necessary. A potent medication can be prepared by the process already mentioned. Once the first result is achieved and understood, further investigation will continue to reveal more and more of the secrets in Alchemy. These can only be experienced personally and individually by each student.

For those not able to procure an extraction apparatus, another method may be used which is much simpler in regards to the equipment needed. This was originally described in the Alchemical Laboratory Bulletin, 1st Quarter, No. 1, 1960 and is repeated in the material which follows.

This is intended for those who have studied or read about Alchemy and are now preparing themselves to commence work in the laboratory. As this will prove to be a most interesting and enlightening task, it should not be undertaken carelessly. First of all, the selection of a proper place for the work about to begin is of importance. The space required is not large. A corner in the basement, or in an attic, perhaps even a garage will do, as long as a constant source of heat is available. Cold water should also be close by for the cooling of the condenser tube. A few bottles and flasks and a mortar and pestle are desirable, if not necessary.

A table and a chair complete the furnishings. The table or work-bench should be so located that the heat and water source are very close by, as the gas flame or electric heat (whichever is used) is constantly needed. For the gas flame, a Bunsen burner, or better still, a Fisher burner is recommended. Erlenmeyer flasks, those with the flat bottoms, is the type best for our purposes. As for stoppers, both the rubber and cork types are needed. A small mixed assortment will last a long time. A support to hold the flask over the flame, and to maintain it in a rigid position when distillation is taking place is also required. It can either be bought or made by the student, as long as it meets the requirements.

Since the most important implements are by now known to the beginner, we shall now continue by preparing the substance with which we are going to work alchemically. Let us choose an herb that is easily available—for example, Melissa (Melissa officinalis-Lemon-balm). Since it is an important herb and any supply house can furnish it, we shall use it as an example in our first experiment.

As mentioned previously, it is preferable in the beginning to use the dried herb. At this point we should ascertain if we have actually selected the desired herb. This may seem unnecessary, but it is quite important. There is, for instance, a difference between wild and garden sage in our work. The flowers of the wild sage, again, will produce a different medication than the leaves from the same plant. Therefore, the student must always be certain that the herbal substance involved is the desired one.

The next step in the procedure is the grinding of the herb. This may be accomplished by rubbing between the hands or by grinding it in a mortar with a pestle. The more minute the particles the easier the extraction. The ground herb is now placed in a flask, bottle, or container (preferably glass) that can be well closed. Over the ground herb the menstruum is now poured which will produce the extraction. The easiest way is to pour some strong alcohol (NEVER use denatured alcohol or Methanol), or preferably brandy, over the ground herb in the flask or bottle. Then it should be closed tightly and put on top or near the furnace in the winter. If warmth is provided by some other method, the temperature should not exceed that required for the hatching of chicken eggs. One-half to one-third of the container should be left empty above the menstruum, in order that it will have room for expansion and to relieve some of the pressure that may build up within the container.

After several days, the menstrum will be colored green. The shade of green will depend on the type of melissa used and the strength and purity of the alcohol. When sufficiently macerated (this process is called maceration), the liquid is to be poured off into a clean glass container. The remaining herbal substance should be placed in a calcining dish and burnt to ashes. The alcohol which has saturated the herb will ignite immediately and burn the remainder of the herb, now called "feces," to black ashes. As this will cause smoke and a strong odor, care should be taken not to do this in a closed room.

After the burning of the feces, as we shall now call them, they can be incinerated in any fire-resistant dish until they become a light gray. An occasional grinding in the mortar followed by further burning, which we shall now call "calcination," will gradually bring about a lighter color. When this state has been reached the feces should be removed from the fire and, while still warm, placed into a flask which has been preheated, so that it will not break from the sudden temperature change. Into this flask is poured the essence which had been previously poured off of the macerated herb and put aside. Now the flask must be tightly stoppered so that no alcohol fumes can escape. The flask then is subjected to moderate heat for digestion. Left to digest in this way for an interval of two weeks, the Salt will absorb the Essence necessary for the formation of the required strength. The medication is then ready for use. It is absolutely harmless but of high potency and should be taken in minute amounts. A few grains of the Salt together with a teaspoon of the liquid Essence in a glass of distilled water will produce exhilarating results. The elixir should never be consumed undiluted. This is the most primitive and simplest form of preparing an herbal substance according to the precepts of Alchemy.

The time during the maceration period can be put to beneficial use in producing a pure menstruum from alcohol or spirits of wine. While there are various kinds of alcohol, only one is of interest to us at the outset of our work. This is the spirit of wine. As wine generally contains less than 20% alcohol by natural fermentation, this alcohol (spirit of wine) must be extracted. Since we are interested only in alcohol extracted from grape wine, we must exclude all other types of wines—apple wine, loganberry wine, etc.

Our next step, then, is to take pure unadulterated grape wine or brandy and pour a sufficient amount into a flask for distillation. The amount depends upon the flask at hand. It should never be filled more than half full. Two holes should then be drilled through a rubber or cork stopper. Through these a thermometer in one and a bent glass tube in the other must fit tightly. The thermometer should not touch the wine, while the bent glass tube reaches barely below the stopper. Now a condenser is needed. This may be purchased from any chemical supply house. The bent glass tube from the flask must be inserted into the stopper closing the condenser opening.

What has been formed now is known as a distillation train. In order to keep the condenser cool with water, it must be connected by means of a rubber tube to a water tap. Most likely an adapter will be needed for this purpose. The water will flow to the condenser jacket and then out at the top opening through another rubber tube and then into a drain. In this way, the vapor that rises from the heated flask will be cooled and will drip out from the bottom end of the condenser into a receptacle.

Once the heat under the flask is started and the wine begins to boil, a vapor will rise and pass through the bent glass tube and then enter the condenser. Here the cooling water around the inner tube will cause it to condense and emerge at the end as a distillate, dripping into a receiver. The heat should be so regulated that the first distillation will not exceed 80 degrees centigrade. A thermometer will indicate whether the heat must be increased or decreased in order to maintain this temperature.

When about 15 drops have been distilled over and the temperature has been regulated so that the thermometer shows the same degree of heat, the receiver may be attached to the condenser end. This is done in order to avoid any unnecessary evaporation of the alcohol or any possible ignition of its fumes. This, however, should be done only after the pressure in the distillation train has become equalized. This will be after some of the liquid has come over. When the temperature begins to rise above 85°C. and all of the alcohol has come over, there will still be some traces of water in the alcohol. When the flame has been extinguished and the vessels are cool enough to handle, the train may then be disconnected.

The residue of the wine may now be discarded as it is of no further use to us at present. However, the distillate is saved. But as this distilled spirit of wine is not pure as yet, it must undergo several further distillations in order to become absolute alcohol. At this point we should be certain that the quantity of distillate we have to work with exceeds 100 ml. Each redistillation is accomplished in the same way as the first distillation. As each distillation is completed, the distillate is poured back into a dry distillation flask. During these subsequent distillations, the temperature must be approximately 78°C. At the end of each distillation there will always remain a small amount of cloudy residue which must be discarded as it contains water. Only during the last distillation (approximately seven distillations are sufficient) should the temperature be 76°C. As this final menstruum contains no more traces of water, it reaches the spiritual essence of an herb in a shorter time and more effectively than before it was completely rectified.

Another method to purify spirits of wine is by using potassium carbonate anhydrous. However, in the beginning we do not use this process.

The purified spirits of wine enable us to achieve superior results for herbal extraction. Therefore, we shall always use it in our herbal work.

In a German book it reads as follows in a condensed version.*

---

* From: Grossman: Die Pflanze im Zauberglauben und in der spagyrischen (okkulten) Heilkunst. Verlag Karl Sigismund, Berlin, 1922.

Fifty pounds of a fresh, flowering plant including root, stem, leaves and seeds are cleaned from dying leaves and other impurities and then washed. After cutting the plant into small pieces, water is poured over it and then slowly distilled. Any oil that shows is separated from the water and the water thus obtained without the oil, which is by now kept separate, is poured back over the plant to which has been added one to two spoons of yeast. All of this is placed in a wooden container and slightly covered so it can ferment. One has to watch that when the fermentation has ceased that it is stirred well, placed in a distillation flask and distilled until nothing more distills over. A steam distillation is best. What remains in the flask is calcined, leached out with water, filtered and the filtrate slowly evaporated. The residue is saved. The former distillate is reduced by further distillation until two parts of distillate come to one part of the leached out salt. Both are distilled once more and the oil separated from the first distillation is now added.

Dried, not poisonous plants should be finely pulverized and with six parts water digested for 3 - 4 days in a warm place. Then the entire process mentioned before is repeated.

The well-known M.D. and Ph.D. Zimpel says in his "Taschenrezeptierbuch fuer Spagyriker" (Pocket prescriptionbook for Spagyrists) in part: After collecting wildgrowing flowering medicinal herbs or their respective medicinal parts and cutting them into small pieces, a special yeast is added and everything subjected to fermentation. This fermentation yields the peculiarities of the plant and frees the ethereal oils. After fermentation the newly formed alcohol is carefully distilled. The residue dried and calcined and the calcined salt leached out with the distillate. The liquor thus obtained is filtered—which contains the soluble minerals of the medicinal plant including its essence and volatile oil. The longer it is left undisturbed before using, the better—like wine when left to "ripen" in the bottle is suposedly to increase its efficacy.

As can be seen from the two examples cited there is little difference except Dr. Zimpel leaches his salt right way with its first distillate.

Such minor differences here and there will be found all over in alchemical literature. It is up to the practitioner to find his own way which only experience will teach.

A Basement Laboratory — Concealed from the curious, husband and wife share the marvels of Divine creative unfoldment in the quiet hours of the evening and sometimes late at night. Accumulated over a lengthy period of time, it can be considered a model alchemical laboratory. Covered by the flasks is the waterbath. Not shown are, in the furnace room, the flasks put there for digestion.

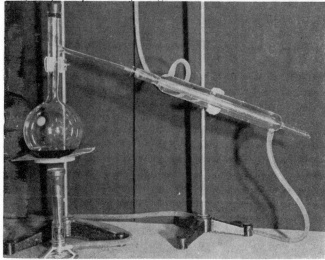

A Distillation Train — At the bottom is the burner; above it are the distilling flask and condenser connected to sidearm. The hose at the bottom brings the water into the condenser walls. Water leaves the condenser through the upper hose. Two supports, each holding an instrument, complete the apparatus necessary for distillation.

Essential Equipment—From left to right: Beaker, Erlenmeyer flasks, Cylinder (for measuring), and Funnel. These items are in constant use in the laboratory.

The illustration above shows a distillation train before the condenser is connected to the distilling flask. Note the thermometer inserted through the stopper hole in top of flask. Funnel in Erlenmeyer flask acts as receptacle for distillate.

Chapter IV

MEDICINAL USES

In all our investigations of nature we must observe what quantities or doses of the body is requisite for a given effect; and must guard ourselves from estimating it at too much or too little.

—*Francis Bacon*

Ailments differs as do the individuals who suffer from them. Hardly any bodily disorder can be standardized and, therefore, we must be very careful in prescribing the exact doses of either tincture, extract, salt, or the combined medication. Since we are chiefly concerned here with alchemical elixirs (the combination of Essence, Sulphur and Salt), it is well to mention again that a more potent medication is obtained each time we repeat the process of calcination and coagulation, after the first state has been attained.

Distilled water and spirits of wine are the two common mediums used for the dissolving of the herbal elixir. If the elixir has been properly prepared, it will dissolve without trouble in either liquid. It should never be taken full strength in such large amounts as a teaspoonful, etc. Due to the condensed potency and accelerated vibratory rate of the herbal elixir, it must be taken greatly diluted. A few grains may be dissolved in a glassful of water or pure unadulterated red wine. Two or three tablespoonfuls taken at hourly intervals will usually produce the desired results, provided the ailment has been properly diagnosed and the patient's condition is known. If this cannot be done personally, the experience of a physician should be called upon. His diagnosis and prescribed medication should be carefully ascertained. If his prescription contains an herbal substance as the main ingredient, this is to be used. In other words, from this herb an alchemical preparation is to be produced. However, great care must be taken that the basic medication is not a poisonous one. A sedative, for instance, acts as an opiate and not as a curative agent. If a patient requests his physician to recommend an herbal medication, the true physician will certainly comply, if the case warrants it. Likewise, no true physician will deny his patient information leading to a cure, if this is known to him, of course.

We are dealing chiefly with herbs in this book; therefore, only prescriptions containing herbs as basic ingredients have been referred to. Medications of a mineral or metallic nature have not been mentioned in detail. It should have become obvious to the reader that alchemical preparations must be individually prepared, as they are not obtainable in drug or apothecary stores. Such alchemical herbal preparations are taken until relief from the ailment is noticed, which the herb in question is supposed to help cure. If for any reason the herbal elixir does not cure the ailment, or at least bring relief from pain, then it is evident that a state of disorder prevails in which herbal preparations do not have sufficiently strong enough vibrations to eliminate the disorder and restore a harmonious balance. In such a case, it would be necessary to use the next highest medication, but which is to be found outside the herbal realm.

It is unreasonable to expect an herbal elixir to bring about an immediate result in every case. The manifestation of any cure will depend upon the length of time the ailment has been present and the state of its progress in the disruption of organic functions. Very important, also, is the state of mind of the patient. While an herbal elixir is not a cure-all, it is definitely of greater curative potency than the tincture and salts taken separately. Through Alchemy that which has been violated is restored, and nature is helped to reach the state of perfection which is the predestined goal for all its manifestations. A sick body is not in a normal or perfect state. However, to force a cure is just as contrary to nature as contracting an illness. Alchemy provides a perfect medium through which that state of perfection or harmonious balance can be gained again. Nature requires a certain period of time for the production of her specimen. This is also true of the alchemist in his laboratory, but here the time intervals are relatively shorter. Therefore, the time required *to cure an ailment and not just to bring about a temporary relief from pain* depends upon the seriousness of the individual conditions. A recent illness which has been contracted over a short period of time will yield more quickly to our alchemical preparations than one which has developed into a chronic state. However, fresh air, normal physical exercise, proper food, adequate clothing, as well as satisfactory sanitary and working conditions are equally essential for curative purposes.

Beginning spagyric practitioners inevitably wonder why it is necessary to deal with herbal Alchemy when it is well known to all that medications prepared from herbs are less potent than those prepared from minerals and metals. However, it is essential that alchemists-to-be understand that nature's laws are unfolded only gradually. That which has been learned in working with the herbal process can be applied later to the work with metals. But the higher arcanum should not be attempted until the herbal process has been mastered. There is much that must be learned which only personal experience in the laboratory and the wisdom of the Sages and Adepts can help to unfold. Eventually, time alone will tell.

Although the process for obtaining alchemical herbal elixirs, as presented here, appears to be extremely simple, much experience is still necessary before the first correct results greet the beginning alchemist's eyes. Even then, the very small amount of the alchemical preparation which is finally produced may seem so insignificant to the beginner that he may then be filled with doubts and wonder if all the work and trouble was really worthwhile. It is only after the first manifestation reveals itself, after the first cure becomes obvious beyond a doubt that an inner conviction begins to grow that there is more to be found in the realm of Alchemy than meets the eye at first glance.

Before administering any alchemical medication to animals or sick individuals, a test should be performed to determine if the medicine has been properly prepared. This is done by placing a small amount of the prepared herbal substance on a thin sheet of heated copper. If the medication melts like wax and does not give off any smoke, and then solidifies when cold again, it is an indication that the medication has been prepared correctly and that it is ready for use. The correct dosage differs in almost every case, but if administered in small doses there cannot be harm in any case. The strength of the alchemical medication would also be a factor in determining the proper dosage to administer. Alchemical herbal medications are essence and salt in their purest form, as all irrelevant and extraneous matter has been removed during the process of calcination. That which is essential cannot be destroyed by fire, but is only purified and brought to its preordained state. Properly prepared herbal medications in correct doses, because of their raised vibrations, help to right bodily disorders. This vital life force plus its purified salt, or mineral substance, are the curative agents.

That the alchemical system works differently and more efficiently than others is illustrated by the following incident. The writer knows from personal experience of the case of a baby suffering from severe colic. Constant medical attention from an allopathic physician and surgeon brought no relief. However, after administering an alchemical preparation made from the flowers of camomile, the child was cured within a few hours and remained so with no recurrence of the ailment. Critics may object by answering that if proper care had been given to the child from the time the disturbance first began to appear, the original medical attention would also have helped. In this case, though, it must be pointed out that all the medical advice was very painstakingly followed in every detail, and the herbal preparation was accepted only as a last resort in order that the mother and the child might have some sleep after several frantic, sleepless nights. This case is mentioned here only to demonstrate the harmless nature of these preparations to the human body, even to infants, when properly administered. It is highly recommended that the medical profession also make it its study to discover the truth about Alchemy.

If one has had insufficient schooling or is not endowed with a profound desire to study the human anatomy and its related physical functionings, he would hardly find it worthwhile to experiment in herbal Alchemy, let alone to attempt to cure when his knowledge is insufficient because of the long study and tedious work by which this knowledge can only be acquired.

May Bacon's statement close this chapter as it began it: "In all our investigations of nature we must observe what quantity or dose of the body is requisite for a given effect; and must guard ourselves from estimating it at too much or too little."

Chapter V

HERBS AND STARS

How are herbs related to the stars? Can such a thing be true? Scientists will shake their heads in disgust. "Nonsense. Superstition. Quack.", they will answer. And why not? How could scientists accept the possibility of something when at the same time they did not consider it worthy of their efforts to investigate the subject? Or perhaps they might deem it beneath their dignity to "dabble with silly superstitions." The writer may seem rash in his judgment concerning the attitude science has shown toward this branch of research, but experience has revealed that there is a connection between herbs and the heavenly bodies that adorn the firmament. Science must disprove this, if it can. Observation has also revealed that certain countries are influenced by particular planets, as astrology has long declared. Again, certain plants are found only in certain places. As soon as these plants are transplanted into soil foreign to their nature, they lose all or some of their curative virtues.

In plant and mineral life, organic and inorganic minerals exist as separate groups. In this plant and mineral life, all growth gives evidence of an unseen but measurable change in proportion to its structure. What causes this growth? Inorganic minerals are taken up into plant life and changed into organic minerals. What brings this change about? Radium is able to cause a decay of tissues. Is it radium as substance or the unseen but measurable emanation from a mysterious force from within? Science asks us to believe that the structure of the radium atom is like a cosmos in miniature. A solar system in Microcosmos. A layman who is unable to verify scientific theories must either believe or not believe them. That one has accepted as natural law what science has propounded should not make

it any more difficult to believe that the Macrocosmos has the same
influence both on the surface as well as below the surface (tissue)
of the earth. Is this so unreasonable? Does not the old hermetic
axiom, "As above so below, as below so above," again have its
counterpart here?

Perhaps science someday will take the time to investigate in these
uncharted areas and experiment on a far broader base than has been
the case so far. While it is true that some scientists have accomplished
remarkable results working in these areas, they have been few and
have been shunned by their colleagues. They attempted to venture
into the unknown, the ridiculed spheres, and have been termed
mystics, heretics, and stray sheep from the herd. All this they were,
but had they not left the beaten path and ventured to explore in other
directions, their labor never would have produced results of alchemical importance.

The following is a condensed tabulation[1] of herbs listed according
to the planetary influence which affects each of them, as claimed by
ancient tradition. In order that this list be of benefit, each student
must discover individually how true these planetary attributions are
for these various herbs. It would seem that even a deeper study is
necessary in order to discover the underlying causes of the different
ways in which the medicinal virtues operate. Many, however, who
have given some thought to this subject will find here a significant
clue.

SUN
angelica
ash tree
bay tree
burnet
butterbur
camomile
celandine
small centaury
eyebright
juniper
lovage
marigold
pimpernel
rosemary
rue
saffron
St. John's wort
St. Peter's wort
sundew

---

[1] See appendix for further details.

tormentil
turnsole
heart-trefoil
vine viper's bugloss
walnut tree

MOON
adder's tongue
arrach
brankursine
colewort
water caltrop
chickweed
clary
cleavers
coralwort
water cress
cucumber
duckmeat
fleur de lys
(or water flag)
fluellein
cuckoo-flower
lettuce
water-lily
white lily
loosestrife
moonwort
mouse-ear
orpine
pellitory of Spain
rattle-grass
saxifrage
stonecrop
pearl-trefoil
wallflower
willow tree

MERCURY
bitter-sweet
calamint
wild carrot
caraway
dill
elecampane
fern
fennel
germander
hazelnut
horehound
houndstongue
lavender
lily of the valley
liquorice
wall rue (or white maiden-hair)
golden maiden-hair
marjoram
mulberry tree
nailwort
oats
parsley
parsnip
pellitory of the wall
sauce-alone (garlic cress)
savory
scabius
smallage
southernwood
honeysuckle
valerian

VENUS
alkanet
alehoof or ground ivy
artichoke
black or common alder tree

wild arrach
archangel bean
bishop's weed
bramble
blites
bugle
burdock
cherry tree
earth chestnuts
chickpease
columbine
coltsfoot
cudweed
cowslip
crab's claw
crosswort
daisy
devil's bit
eringo
featherfew
dropwort
figwort
foxglove
golden rod
gromel
gooseberry
groundsel
herb-robert
true-love
kidneywort
ladies' mantle
marshmallow
french mercury
dog mercury
mint
moneywort
motherwort
mugwort

nep or catmint
orchis
parsley piert
parsnip
pennyroyal
pear tree
periwinkle
plantain
plum tree
poppy
purslane
primrose
privet
queen of the meadows
ragwort
rye
woodsage
sanicle
self-heal
soapwort
sorrel
sow-thistle
spignel
strawberry
tansey
teasel
vervain
wheat
yarrow

MARS

all-heal
prunella vulgaris
barberry
basil
briony
benedictus
cardines

crowfoot
dovesfoot
flax-weed
burze bush
garlic
gentian
hawthorn
hedge-hyssop
hop
madder
master-wort
nettle
onion
pepperwort
ground pine
horse radish
rhubarb
savine
star thistle
tobacco
wormwood

JUPITER
agrimony
alexander
wild parsley
asparagus
balm
white beet
bilberry
borage
chervil
chestnut tree
cinque foil
costmary
dandelion
dock
dog's grass

endive
fig tree
clove-gilliflowers
hart's tongue
hyssop
house-leek
livewort
lungwort
maple tree
melilot
oak tree
roses
sage samphire
scurvy-grass
lady's thistle

SATURN
amaranthus
barley
corn
red beet
beech tree
bifoil
birds-foot
blue bottle
buck's horn plantain
comfrey
sciatica-cress
darnel
dodder
elm tree
water-fern
fleawort
flux weed
fumitory
gladwin
goutwort
heart's ease

hawkweed
hemlock
henbane
black hellebore
horsetail
holly
ivy
knapweed
knotgrass
medlar tree
mosses
mullein
nightshade
polypody of the oak
poplar tree

quince tree
service tree
shepherd's purse
spleen-wort
tamarisk tree
melancholy thistle
black thorn
thorough wax
tutsan
woad
Solomon's seal
Saracen's consound
willow herb
winter green
yew tree

In concluding this condensed table of herbs and corresponding planetary influences, it will be interesting to add a few further observations. These can be corroborated by those who wish to do so and who may then arrive at their own personal conclusions.

Is there anyone capable of answering why the chickweed flowers are open and upright from nine in the morning until noon? However, if it rains they remain closed and after the rain they become pendent. The "Four-O-Clock" opens its flower at about four in the afternoon. The dandelion (a true sundial) opens at seven in the morning and closes at five in the afternoon. The pimpernel (the poor man's weatherglass) closes its tiny flowers long before it rains or night draws near. The purple sandworth flower expands only when the sun shines. If the trefoil contracts its leaves, thunder and heavy rains can be expected. Many similar examples could be cited. What causes such variance in behavior? All have their roots in the ground and draw their nourishment from the soil and the air. Yet their behavior is remarkably different. Is it so unreasonable to assume that they, as well as tiny atoms, are governed according to similar laws?

There is no point in going any further into this matter here as sufficient material can be found in the following pages to help in the assimilation of the spiritual essence for further transmutation.

However, a subject related to the planetary influences on plants and herbs does deserve attention. This involves the planetary influences on the various parts of the human body. The zodiac is represented as ruler of the body whose parts are distributed throughout the twelve houses. These, in turn, are ruled by certain planets. A connecting link, therefore, can easily be determined with a minimum of ingenuity by the spagyric student.

The following tabulation, according to Paracelsus, of organs of the body and the respective planets that rule them will be of assistance for further analysis:

> The Sun rules the heart.
> The Moon rules the brain.
> Venus rules the veins.
> Saturn rules the spleen.
> Mercury rules the liver.[1]
> Jupiter rules.the lungs (chest).
> Mars rules the gall.

Since the writings of this great sage, Paracelsus, are of such importance, it is almost essential that students of alchemical literature give his works very careful study.

Paracelsus is in agreement with previous teachers in regard to the fact that the stars influence all growing things. These growing things, then, correspond exactly to the number of influences and stars. But as some trees produce pears and other trees apples, so some stars yield rain, others snow, hail, etc. Thus, in this fashion what falls from heaven is generated.

Paracelsus speaks of the hot and cold nature of ailments and also of remedies falling under these two classifications.[2] In such cases the homeopathic principle of "similia similibus curantur"—like cures like—can be employed. This principle perhaps can best be illustrated

---

[1] Culpeper states that Jupiter rules the liver and Mercury the lungs.

[2] Black pepper (piper niger), mustard (sinapis), nutmeg (nux moschata) for example, are medicaments of a hot nature. Those herbs of the mentha (mint) family are medicaments of a cold nature.

by taking a frozen egg and placing it in cold water. The frost will be drawn out by the cold and the egg will be wholesome again. Since like repels like in physical phenomena, the homeopathic approach of curing, say, arsenic poisoning, is to use the same substance, namely, arsenic. Thus, if a physiological dose of arsenic will bring about arsenic poisoning, the homeopathic practitioner will use this same substance, arsenic, in a most minute or highly triturated form to effect a cure. Here the high trituration causes the arsenic particles to become so small that they can no longer be perceived. Because of the high trituration, the vibratory rate is greatly increased and achieves high potency in expelling the physiological dose of arsenic. Therefore, in homeopathy the identical substance is used to repel an illness which substance in a physiological dose caused the illness in the first place. Perhaps the phrase, "curative dose," is inadequate, but it is being used to convey the process. However, in using highly triturated homeopathic agents, one cannot really speak of a dose since the curative substance is so inconceivably small—1:100,000,000 and even smaller.[1]

Homeopathy is nearer to Alchemy than other therapies, but is still far from producing alchemical actions, inasmuch as it does not set free the quintessence which is so essential as a *healing* agent. Since Homeopathy, as taught by Hahnemann, is only a segment of Paracelsian therapeutics and is comparatively little used, what can one expect as to the acceptance of Herbal Alchemy?

Alchemically a cure is obtained by using the opposing forces of negative against positive. An ailment presents the negative aspect while curative agents represent positive forces. Manifestations occur where these opposite forces meet. The object of alchemical remedies is to supplement the lacking or deficient positive forces in the human body which represents the negative part in contradistinction to the positive vital life force (which in Sanskrit is called "prana").[2] This

---

[1] Prof. Liebig in his chemical letters said: "The smaller the particles of a prescribed medicine the less physical resistance they met in their diffusion in the tissue."

[2] Dr. Schuessler's system of biochemistry prescribes the 12 tissue remedies to build up the missing minerals in the blood. Homeopathy differs from biochemistry, the first curing like with like and biochemistry replenishing or build-

vital life force, prana, or quintessence can only be separated through Alchemy. It is this difference, the separation of the quintessence, that sets Alchemy on a higher level above all other systems of therapeutics.

If it is true, as has been claimed, that the heavenly bodies radiate an unseen power that has been observed to manifest differently among the various specimens of the herbal kingdom, only an investigation by sincere and unprejudiced students is needed to substantiate these observations.

---

ing up lacking minerals in the blood. Both homeopathy and biochemistry have a closer relationship with alchemical therapeutics than the administering of physiological doses according to the allopathic system. However, even allopathic physicians are attenuating their doses now in what is known as serum therapy. This is only an indication of a further step by modern medicine to approach nearer to the only perfect natural system of healing which is to be found in Alchemy.

If any of Dr. Schuessler's tissue remedies, such as calcium, silica, potassium, etc. were to be separated into its three essentials (according to alchemical practice), namely, sulphur, salt, and mercury, and then coagulated again, it is not difficult to imagine the potential remedies that could be obtained in this fashion. Such remedies would truly replenish and build up the body due to the raised vibrations of these remedies. This holds true also of any of the homeopathic preparations, which is to say their basic substance before trituration with lactose (milksugar) or spirits of wine. However, neither system frees the quintessence, the most important matter in alchemical preparations.

What is essential can not be destroyed by fire. Out of the Cosmic retort rises the vital life force to let the Qabalistic Tree of Life grow, so that the Alchemist may partake of its fruit and thereby obtain eternal life, light and love.

Chapter VI

SYMBOLS IN ALCHEMY

Mysterious symbols have intrigued the mind of man from time immemorial. In every epoch, religion, magic and alchemy have abounded in the use of symbols. Meanings of diverse kinds and interpretations bordering on the hallucinatory and fantastic have been attributed to these strange signs. One can understand, then, if even today, such expressions as "signs of the devil," "marks of the devil," etc., can still be found among various peoples. In alchemy, nothing devilish or unholy is concealed behind these symbols. On the contrary, to those who are able to understand them, they possess an honorable and even a holy significance. This understanding has been considered too sacred and too valuable to be cast before the unworthy. Alchemists, and especially the Rosicrucian fraters, have used these sacred symbols amongst themselves in order to prevent alchemical, mystical, or occult secrets from falling into the hands of those who would misuse them. Rosicrucian adepts were known to have secret powers and methods to accomplish what seemed miraculous to others, as has been recorded for centuries. For example, the wonderful work (In German) of W. G. Surya, *Der Stein der Weisen (The Stone of the Wise)*, presents an almost unbelievable but authentic record of these sages during past centuries. Even today, the very same symbols are employed by the alchemical brethren whenever necessary.

The occasion may arise for the alchemist-to-be, now reading these pages, when he may come in contact with books and manuscripts containing these alchemystical symbols. For this reason, the following pages present the important signs together with their Latin and English names. To some, such symbols are of little importance now, but they will prove of immense value when, at the least suspected time, a connecting link will present itself. Members of the age-old fraternity of Rosicrucians are still very actively engaged in alchemy as part of their occult and mystical work. However, one must discriminate between pseudo-Rosicrucians who may outwardly belong to one of several organizations making use of that name, and real adepts who comprise the inner core of the circle of the Order, which still exists throughout the Occident and the Orient. As previously stated, it would be useless to attempt to locate or even to contact this inner circle. It is true that Rosicrucian alchemical symbols have been published prior to their appearance here, and no doubt they will find their way into print again in the future. Such symbols are always of interest to students of occultism and mysticism. They are included in this little work only to help students arrive at a fundamental understanding of their basic meanings. For this reason, they are compiled in a condensed, yet comprehensive, way.

No claim is made that the symbols reproduced here are the only ones used in alchemy. Basilius Valentinus employed some of similar design plus others entirely of his own composition. Some alchemists devised their own sets of symbols when it became apparent that formerly used signs had fallen into the hands of charlatans, who only made use of them to defraud and deceive the public.

Regarding individual interpretation of alchemical symbols, it can only be said that an inner unfoldment will help the student alchemist to arrive at their correct meanings. The profound message they contain will never be fully explained in the printed word nor in the attempted translations of "schooled intellectuals."

The symbols as used by the Rosicrucian fraters are given here in such a way that interpretation is superfluous. They are presented in the same manner that a dictionary define certain words and phrases.

ROSICRUCIAN ALCHEMY

I SIGNS OF ELEMENTS

△   Ignis—Fire

⟁   Aer—Air

▽   Aqua—Water

⩒   Terra—Earth

II SIGNS OF METALS AND PLANETS

☿   Argentum vivum—Mercury

♃   Stannum (Jupiter)—Tin

♀   Cuprum (Venus)—Copper

☽   Argentum (Luna)—Silver

☉   Sol—Gold

♂   Ferrum (Mars)—Iron

♄   Plumbum (Saturn)—Lead

III SIGNS OF MINERALS

Antimonium—Antimony

Sulphur—Sulphur

Cinabris—Cinnabar

Lithargirium—Lead Monoxide

Talcum—Tale

Marcasit—Marcasite

Magnet—Magnet, Lodestone

Arsenicum—Arsenic

Aurum pigmentum—Gold pigment

Alumen—Aluminium

Nitrum—Soda

Sal—Salt

⊖   Salprapuratum—Saltpeter

℞   Vitriolum—Vitriol

C   Calx—Lime, Chalk

⊕   Viride Aeris—Green of Copper (CopperChlate)

Ψ   Calcovviva—Quick lime

∴   Arena—Sand

IV PRODUCTS OF MINERALS

     Aurichalcum—Orichalchum or Brass

     Specular—Glass of Talc or Hematite (Slate Ore or Stone-Mica)

     Mercurius Sublimatus—Refined Mercury

     Mercurius praecipitatus—Amalgam or Mercury Solid

    Regulus—Pure Metal

    Limatura Martis—Iron Filings

    Tutia—Zinc Carbonate or Oxide

    Miny—Red Lead Oxide

    Cerussa—Lead Acetate

    Flores—Oxdide of a Metal

    Attramentum—Black Ink

     Mercurius vita—Pure Mercury—Quicksilver

V SIGNS OF VEGETABLES

Tartarus—Potassium Bitartrate

Saltartari—Potassium Carbonate

Cinis—Ashes

Cinceres Clavellati—Crude Potassium—Carbonate

Lixivium—Liquor

Acetum—Vinegar

Acetum Distillatum—Distilled Vinegar

Spiritus—Alcohol Solution

Spiritus vini—Spirits of Wine

Spiritus vini Root—Rectified spirits of wine

Cera—Wax

Sacharum—Sugar

Camphor—Camphor

Herba—Herb

Radices—Roots

Gumi—Gum

VI SIGNS OF ANIMALS

Urina—Urine

Cornua Cervi—Hart's Horn—Ammonium Carbonate

Cancer—Crab

♌   Leo—Lion

♍   Virgo—Virgin

♎   Simia, Libra—Ape

♏   Scorpio—Scorpion

♐   Archbearer—Archbearer

♑   Caper—Goat, Capricorn

♒   Amphora—Pitcher, Vase;—Measure

♓   Pisces—Fish

♊   Gemini—Twins

♉   Taurus—Bull

♈   Ares—Ram

VII SIGNS OF TIME

♊   Annus—Year

⊠   Mensis—Month

♉   Hora—Time

♂   Dies—Day

♀   Nox—Night

VIII SIGNS OF WEIGHT

℔   Libra—Scales—Pound

℥   Uncia—Ounce

℥ss   Uncia Semis—Half Ounce

ʒ   Drachma—⅛ Ounce

ʒss   Drachma ½—1/16 Ounce

Scrupulus—1/24 Ounce (20 grms.)

Scrupulus ½—1/48 Ounce

Grana—Grain

Gutta—Drop

Ana—Equal Parts of Each

Quantum Satis—Sufficient Quantity

Manipulus—Handful

IX SIGNS OF INSTRUMENTS

Alembicum Vitrum—Glass Container

Retorta—Retort

Vas recipiens—Receiver

Crucibulus—Crucible

Balneum Mariae—Water Bath

Balneum Vaporis—Steam Bath

Ignis Circulator—Furnace

X SIGNS OF OPERATION

Sublimare—Sublimate

Precipitare—Precipitate

Filtrare—Filter

Amalgamare—Amalgamate

Digestio—To heat in water or digest in moderate heat

Ƨ   Luto. Lutrine—Mud of Otter

≋   Solvere—Solution

∫∫∫   Stratum Super Stratum—Layer upon Layer

Ƒ   Extrahere—Extract

ℛ   Distillare—Distill

Ɣ   Evaporare—Evaporate

XI SIGNS OF VARIOUS PRODUCTS

∞   Oleum—Oil

Λ   Volatile—Not Fixed, Active

V   Fixum—Fixed

⊕   Caput mortum—Dead Head

✶   Ammoniatum—Ammonia

◇   Salpo—Potassium Sulphate

⌂   Borax—Sodium Biborate

℘   Crystalli—Crystals

○╫╫   Pulvis—Dust

XII ALCHEMICAL CIPHERS

+ I _ L ⌐ ⌐ ⌐ I− ┤ T ⊥ ⇐ ⇒ V Λ ⋝ ⋞ ≺ ≻ ≻ ⋜ Y ⋀
1 2 3 4 5 6 7 8 9 10 11 12 13 14 15 16 17 18 19 20 21 22 23

I Z Ƨ Ƴ Ƨ ⋀ 7 Ⴆ ⋎ Ƅ I Z Ƨ Ƴ Ƨ Ⴑ 7 ⋎ ⋎ Ⴆ ⋎ Z Ƨ Ƨ
1 2 3 4 5 6 7 8 9 10 11 12 13 14 15 16 17 18 19 20 21 22 23 24

CHAPTER VII

WISDOM OF THE SAGES

(The Work Upon the Metals)

RESUMÉ OF A ROSICRUCIAN CONVENTION, 1777

The following alchemical material was obtained from a rare manuscript handwritten in Latin and German script and Rosicrucian ciphers. The four sections of the original document are arranged as follows: A - Introduction; I - First Degree; II - Second Degree; III - Third Degree. This work, together with the first edition of *The Secret Symbols of the Rosicrucians,* was brought to this country by the widow of a Mr. Ernst Klatscher, a native of Prague, Czechoslovakia Mr. Klatscher was a high degree Mason, who had been interested in Rosicrucianism for some years. The invasion of his country during World War II forced Mr. Klatscher and his family into exile. They fled in such haste that only their most highly prized possessions could be carried with them. Among these were *The Secret Symbols of the Rosicrucians* and the document we summarize here.

Naturally, this manuscript is priceless. The original came from a monastery in Prague (in the country formerly known as Bohemia), for many years the center of alchemical activity. As far as we are able to determine, the original of this document no longer exists. Perhaps these photostats alone survive. A.E. Waite, in his book, *The Brotherhood of the Rosy Cross,* (p. 457) mentions that he knew of the existence of this document as recorded in a Rosicrucian Convention held in Germany in 1777. The photostats in our possession include an outline of the entire studies, ritual, and especially the alchemical work as used by the Rosicrucians of that day.

65

The Rosicrucian Order, AMORC, obtained these photostatic copies and the first edition of *The Secret Symbols of the Rosicrucians* from the executor of the state of Ernst Klatscher. Mr. Klatscher died either on his way to America or immediately after he arrived here. His widow turned over these documents to Frenkel and Company, an old established firm having offices in London, Paris, Amsterdam, and Hamburg.

The *Introduction,* itself, is divided into three parts of three reports each. The total number of pages in the introduction is thirty-five. The first report covers pages 1 to 22, the second pages 23 to 28, and the third, which seems to deal more or less with alchemical notes, pages 29 to 35. The report of the First Degree, Junior Degree, or Zelators as they are called, contains nine pages. In addition to this, there are four large tables, two of four pages each and the other two of two pages each. One of these tables, Number 4, is extremely valuable from an alchemical point of view, as it contains all of the symbols used by the Rosicrucians of all ages in their alchemical work.

The *First Degree* gives instruction concerning the four alchemical elements and the symbols by which they are represented. Other Qabalistic material in relation to Alchemy is given, dating back even to the time of Solomon. The relationship of the triangle, signifying the beginning, middle, and end, and its other correspondences to divine names is the reason that the triangle was adopted, with slight alterations, to represent the four elements. One who understands thoroughly these principles of the four elements can bring forth from them the alchemical Salt, Sulphur, and Mercury. Later on the student is taught how to unite this Salt, Sulphur, and Mercury in a higher degree. The fundamental law of the Order is given in this degree to be the pursuance of wisdom and virtue, rather than to abide in the the domain of mammon when the philosopher's stone is discovered. This is thoroughly impressed upon each member of this degree. The instruction of the higher members, the members' own initiative and energy, and the mercy of God will determine whether or not they will ever make a transmutation.

Incidentally, it is also specified that the cost of experiments undertaken is to be controlled and restricted to such a degree that the material possessions of members will not be depleted. Members are expected to work together in groups and to supplement each other's work, thereby reducing the cost of experiments. Disobedience of this rule would be punished by such penalties as suspension or expulsion from the Order.

The *Second Degree,* or that of the Fratres Theoricus, has five pages. The fifth page has the cipher of the degree. (In these manuscripts, instead of being called First, Second, and Third Degrees, the different stages are named First, Second, and Third Classes-or Zelators, Fratres Theoricus, etc.) The Fratres of this degree or class were concerned with theory of instruction in direct preparation for the next degree. They may formulate their own theories and slightly change the wording of the instruction so that they may better understand it, but they are not allowed to use any apparatus.

The works of Basil Valentine, Paracelsus, Henry Madathanas, Arnold de Villanova, Raymund Lully, and several anonymous alchemical writers were recommended to members of this degree for careful study. The members assembled together and discussed these authors as they read them. The philosophical heart of the theory of Alchemy, as taught, applied itself to the spiritual world in this manner: It was the fire of love that prepared the heavenly quintessence and eternal tincture of all souls. The definite Rosicrucian instruction concerning the seven planets and the particular metal under the respective influence of each planet was given in detail. In this way were the members of this degree prepared for the next which was a practical one of experimentation. By this time they should have been prepared, as far as theory was concerned, fully comprehending Rosicrucian principles of Alchemy. They must also have a knowledge of the different processes and manipulations in order to obtain the essence from the mineral, vegetable, and animal kingdoms. They had to be familiar with the various minerals and rocks, ores and metals, and be able to obtain pure virgin metal from ore. They should also know the different types of vessels on sight and know for what use they were intended.

The *Third Degree,* or that of Practicus, contains sixteen pages. It is divided into two parts. The first part deals with the alchemical instructions or "Necessary Preparatory Processes for the Philosophical Work." There are four chapters concerning the materials to be obtained, the room, the type of equipment, and the other arrangements of the laboratory. Chapter 5 begins with the actual work. It is titled "How the Radical or Universal Menstruum Resolventia Must Be Prepared from Mineral, Vegetable, and Animal Materials."

Process I deals with the mineral radical menstruum, or just plain metals and precious stones. In brief, it is this: One is to take equal parts of saltpeter and vitriol and purify this with water. The water is then driven off and evaporated and the remaining salts are calcined. A special kind of vitriol is required which should have come from some place outside of Europe, preferably the East Indies, Japan, or Mexico. This was probably due to the fact the copper sulphate in these countries was much stronger than that found in Europe. A complicated process of sublimation and distillation, similar to that described in Cockren's work, next takes place with these salts. The essence thus obtained has the property and power, when mixed with other metals or their salts, of extracting their essence.

Process II is that of preparing the vegetable radical menstruum. Of the vegetable or herb used, one takes the best kind. This is placed in weak acetic acid and rectified spirits of wine. Equal parts of both liquids are to be used. This mixture is placed in an alembic and distilled. It is digested again, and the complete process of mixture and distillation repeated two more times, making a total of three. Finally, as a result of these constant firings, a penitent spirit will come over. There should remain behind, in the alembic, a small amount of dead earth and nitrum (saltpeter). It will then be necessary to make two or three cohobations —i.e., combining the dead earth with the spirit or essence. In this manner, the vegetable radical menstruum is prepared. By placing other herbs in this menstruum, their essential oils can easily be obtained and, thereby, invaluable elixirs and medicaments prepared.

Process III, dealing with the preparation of the animal radical menstruum, begins with the testing of the urine of a healthy person. If the sample is perfectly normal, it is placed in a flask or alembic and distilled. This process is repeated seven times. The remains in the alembic are mixed with the last half of the liquid obtained in the last distillation. This substance is claimed to have an especially powerful effect when applied to sore spots on the human body. The manuscript adds, perhaps humorously, that it is strong enough to freshen up mummies. (Such a preparation may seem repugnant to us today, but many old pharmaceutical, herbal and medical books contain similar practices. In fact, Paracelsus, at one time, confounded and disgusted the medical faculty where he was lecturing by experimenting with the excrement of the human body.)

Process IV, or the preparation of the universal menstruum, begins with the mixture of alcohol and saltpeter, which are then distilled. Taking the combined result, one half pound of nitrum salt is mixed with it in a rubbing manner and distilled again. The resulting combination is mixed with equal portions of the above three results. They, in turn. are distilled and sublimated seven times. The final result will be the universal essence, menstruum, or elixir.

The second part of the Third Degree, beginning on page nine, contains instructions and further elaborations of these four processes. These instructions end with the admonition that all philosophical elixirs, oils, essence, alkahests, and even the Stone, itself, were to be used primarily in the service of mankind and for the glory of God. Of course, those to receive the first benefit would be themselves and other members of the Rosicrucian Order. They were to be chiefly interested in the medicinal values of these preparations, but were to be able to create enough precious stones and metals to maintain the finances of the Order. Stress was again laid upon the fact that all of the ciphers and symbols should be mastered in order that no mistakes would be made. Also, further instructions in spiritual Alchemy were offered to those who had completely mastered the physical Alchemy. We can imagine, therefore, that those who had attained perfect health and financial independence from the world were given a new set of instructions to study and practice in some sequestered spot. There they would probably attain to the highest degree of psychic development and adepthood.

The formulas as given in the manuscript, of course, must not be taken at face value, as they are of necessity concealed in their phraseology. It gives us, however, an interesting glimpse into these groups of sincere students, as well as adepts, who considered their time and effort well spent in order to enter the mystic realm of alchemystical experimentations.

The quotation which follows is from the wisdom of a Sage as recorded in the *Collectanea Chemica*. Its purpose is to help prepare alchemical students for the greater work. It will be recalled by the reader that mention was made that anyone who is able to master the herbal process will find it considerably easier to work with minerals and even metals. Careful study of what follows and prolonged meditation will unlock also this mystery to the one ready to receive it.

"All true philosophers agree that the first Matter of metals is a moist vapour, raised by the action of the central fire in the bowels of the earth, which, circulating through its pores, meets with the crude air, and is coagulated by it into an unctuous water, adhering to the earth, which serves it for a receptacle, where it is joined to a sulphur more or less pure, and a salt more or less fixing, which it attracts from the air, and, receiving a certain degree of concoction from the central and solar heat, is formed into stones and rocks, minerals and metals. These were all formed of the same moist vapour originally, but are thus varied from the different impregnations of the sperm, the quality of salt and sulphur with which it is fixed, and the purity of the earth which serves it for a matrix; for whatever portion of this moist vapour is hastily sublimed to the surface of the earth, taking along its impurities, is soon deprived of its purer parts by the constant action of heat, both solar and central, and the grosser parts, forming a mucilaginous substance, furnish the matter of common rocks and stones. But when this moist vapour is sublimed, very slowly, through a fine earth, not partaking of a sulphureous unctuosity, pebbles are formed; for the sperm of these beautiful, variagated stones, with marbles, alabasters, etc., separates this depurated vapour, both for their first formation and continual growth. Gems are in like manner formed of this moist vapour when it meets with pure salt water, with which it is fixed in a cold place. But if it is sublimed leisurely through places which are hot and pure, where the fatness of sulphur adheres to it, this vapour, which the philosophers call their Mercury, is joined to that fatness and becomes an unctuous matter, which coming afterwards to other places, cleansed by the afore-named vapours where the earth is subtle, pure, and moist, fills the pores of it, and so gold is made. But if the unctuous matter comes into places cold and impure, lead, or Saturn, is produced; if the earth be cold and pure, mixed with sulphur, the result is copper. Silver also is formed of this vapour, where it abounds in purity, but mixed with a lesser degree of sulphur and not sufficiently concocted. In tin, or Jupiter, as it is called, it abounds, but in less purity. In Mars, or iron, it is in a lesser proportion impure, and mixed with an adust sulphur.

"Hence, it appears that the First Matter of metals is one thing, and not many, homogeneous, but altered by the diversity of places and sulphurs with which it is combined. The philosophers frequently describe this matter. Sendivogius calls it heavenly water, not wetting the hands; not vulgar, but almost like rain water. When Hermes calls it a bird without wings, figuring thereby its vaporous nature, it is well described. When he calls the sun its father and the moon its mother, he signifies that it is produced by the action of heat upon moisture. When he says the wind carries it in its belly, he only means that the air is its receptacle. When he affirms that which is inferior is like that which is superior, he teaches that the same vapour on the surface of the earth furnishes the matter of rain and dew, wherewith all things are nourished in the vegetable and animal kingdoms. This now is what the philosophers call their Mercury and affirm it to be found in all things, as it is in fact. This makes some suppose it to be in the human body, others in the dunghill, which has often bewildered such as are fond of philosophical subtleties, and fly from one thing to another, without any fixed theory about what they would seek, expecting to find in the Vegetable or Animal Kingdoms the utmost perfection of the Mineral. To this mistake of theirs, without doubt, the philosophers have contributed with the intention of hiding their First Matter from the unworthy; in which they were, perhaps, more cautious than is necessary, for Sendivogius declares that occasionally, in discourse, he had intimated the art plainly word by word to some who accounted themselves very acute philosophers; but they conceived such subtle notions, far beyond the simplicity of Nature, that they could not, to any purpose, understand his meaning. Wherefore he professes little fear of its being discovered but to those who have it according to the good pleasure and providence of the Most High.

"This benevolent disposition has induced him to declare more openly the First Matter, and fix the artist in his search of it to the mineral kingdom; for, quoting Albertus Magnus, who wrote that in his time grains of gold were found betwixt the teeth of a dead man in his grave, he observes that Albertus could not account for this miracle, but judged it to be by reason of the mineral virtue in man, being confirmed by that saying of Morien: 'And this matter, O King, is extracted from thee.' But this is erroneous, for Morien understood those things philosophically, the mineral virtue residing in its own kingdom, distinct from the animal. It is true, indeed, in the animal kingdom mercury, or humidity, is as the matter, and sulphur, or marrow in the bones, as the virtue; but the animal is not mineral, and *vice versa*. If the virtue of the animal sulphur were not in man, the blood, or mercury, could not be coagulated into flesh and bones; so if there were not a vegetable sulphur in the vegetable kingdom, it could not coagulate water, or the vegetable mercury, into herbs, etc. The same is to be understood in the mineral kingdom.

"These three kingdoms do not, indeed differ in their virtue, nor the three sulphurs, as every sulphur has a power to coagulate its own mercury; and every mercury has a power of being coagulated by its own proper sulphur, and by no other which is a stranger to it.

"Now the reason why gold was found betwixt the teeth of a dead man is this: because in his lifetime mercury had been administered to him, either by unction, turbith, or some other way; and it is the nature of this metal to ascend to the mouth, forming itself an outlet there, to be evacuated with the spittle. If, then, in the time of such treatment, the sick man died, the mercury, not finding an egress, remained in his mouth between his teeth, and the carcass becoming a natural matrix to ripen the mercury, it was shut up for a long time, till it was congealed into gold by its own proper sulphur, being purified by the natural heat of putrefaction, caused by the corrosive phlegm of man's body; but this would never have happened if mineral mercury had not been administered to him.

"All philosophers affirm, with one consent, that metals have a seed by which they are increased, and that this seminal quality is the same in all of them; but it is perfectly ripened in gold only, where the bond of union is so fixed that it is most difficult to decompound the subject, and procure it for the Philosophical Work. But some, who were adepts in the art, have by painful processes taken gold for their male, and the mercury, which they knew how to extract from the less compacted metals, for a female; not as an easier process, but to find out the possibility of making the stone this way; and have succeeded, giving this method more openly to conceal the true confection, which is most easy and simple. We shall, therefore, set before the reader a landmark, to keep him from splitting on this difficulty, by considering what is the seed wherein the metals are increased, that the artist may be no longer at a loss where to seek for it, keeping in view the writings of our learned predecessors on this subject.

"The seed of metals is what the Sons of Wisdom have called their mercury, to distinguish it from quicksilver, which it nearly resembles, being the radical moisture of metals. This, when judiciously extracted, without corrosives, or fluxing, contains in it a seminal quality whose perfect ripeness is only in gold; in the other metals it is crude, like fruits which are yet green, not being sufficiently digested by the heat of the sun and action of the elements. We observed that the radical moisture contains the seed, which is true: yet it is not the seed, but the sperm only, in which the vital principle floats, being invisible to the eye. But the mind perceives it, in a true artists, as a central point of condensed air, wherein Nature, according to the will of God, has included the first principles of life in everything, as well animal and vegetable as mineral; for in animals the sperm may be seen, but not the included principle of impregnation: this is a concentered point, to which the sperm serves only as a vehicle, till, by the action and ferment of the matrix, the point wherein

Nature has included a vital principle expands itself, and then it is perceivable in the rudiments of an animal. So in any esculent fruit (as, for instance, in an apple), the pulp or sperm is much more in proportion than the seed included; and even that which appears to be seed is only a finer concoction of sperm, including the vital stamina; as also in a grain of wheat the flour is only the sperm, the point of vegetation is an included air, which is kept by its sperm from the extremes of cold and heat, till it finds a proper matrix, where the husk being softened with moisture, and warmed by the heat, the surrounding sperm putrefies, making the seed, or concentered air, to expand and to burst the husk carrying along in its motion a milky substance, assimilated to itself from the putrefied sperm. This the condensing quality of the air includes in a film and hardens into a germ, all according to the purpose of Nature.

"If this whole process of Nature, most wonderful in her operations, was not constantly repeated before our eyes, the simple process of vegetation would be equally problematical with that of the philosophers; yet how can the metals increase, nay, how can anything be multiplied without seed? The true artists never pretended to multiply metals without it, and can it be denied that Nature still follows her first appointment? She always fructifies the seed when it is put into a proper matrix. Does she not obey an ingenious artist, who knows her operations, with her possibilities, and attempts nothing beyond them? A husbandman meliorates his ground with compost, burns the weeds, and makes use of other operations. He steeps his seed in various preparations, only taking care not to destroy its vital principle; indeed, it never comes into his head to roast it, or to boil it, in which he shows more knowledge of Nature than some would-be philosophers do. Nature, like a liberal mother, rewards him with a more plentiful harvest, in proportion as he has meliorated her seed and furnished a more suitable matrix for its increase.

"The intelligent gardener goes farther; he knows how to shorten the process of vegetation, or retard it. He gathers roses, cuts salads, and pulls green peas in winter. Are the curious inclined to admire plants and fruits of other climates? He can produce them in his stoves to perfection. Nature follows his directions unconstrained, always willing to obtain her end, viz., the perfection of her offspring.

"Open your eyes here, ye studious searchers of Nature! Is she so liberal in her perishing productions, how much more in those which are permanent, and can subsist in the fire? Attend, then, to her operations; if you procure the metallic seed, and ripen that by art which she is many ages in perfecting, it cannot fail but she will reward you with an increase proportioned to the excellency of your subject.

"The reader will be apt to exclaim here: 'Very fine! All this is well; but how shall the seed of metals be procured, and whence comes it that so few know how to gather it?' To this it is answered that the philosophers have hitherto industriously kept that a profound secret; some out of a selfish disposition, though otherwise good men. Others, who wished only for worthy persons to whom they might impart it, could not write of it openly, because covetousness and vanity have been governing principles in the world; and, being wise men, they knew that it was not the will of the Most High to inflame and cherish such odious tempers, the genuine offspring of pride and self-love, but to banish them out of the earth, wherefore they have been withheld hitherto. But we, finding no restraint on our mind in that respect, shall declare what we know: and the rather because we judge the time is come to demolish the golden calf, so long *had* in veneration by all ranks of men, insomuch that worth is estimated by the money a man possesses; and such is the inequality of possessions that mankind are almost reducible to the rich, who are rioting in extravagance, and the poor, who are in extreme want, smarting under the iron hand of oppression. Now the measure of iniquity among the rich hastens to its limit, and the cry of the poor is come before the Lord: '*Who will give them to eat till they shall be satisfied?*' Hereafter the rich will see the vanity of their possessions when compared with the treasures communicated by this secret; for the riches it bestows are a blessing from God, and not the squeezing of oppression. Besides, its chief excellence consists in making a medicine capable of healing all diseases to which the human body is liable, and prolonging life to the utmost limits ordained by the Creator of all things.

"There want not other reasons for the manifestation of the process; for scepticism has gone hand in hand with luxury and oppression, insomuch that the fundamental truths of all revealed religion are disputed. These were always held in veneration by the possessors of this art, as may be seen from what they have left upon record in their books: and, indeed, the first principles of revealed religion are demonstrated from the whole process, for the seed of metals is sown in corruption, and raised in incorruption; it is sown a natural body, and raised a spiritual body; it is known to partake of the curse which came upon the earth for man's sake, having in its composition a deadly poison, which can only be separated by a regeneration in water and fire; it can, when it is thoroughly purified and exalted, immediately tinge imperfect metals and raise them to a state of perfection, being in this respect a lively emblem of that seed of the woman, the Serpent Bruiser, who, through His sufferings and death, hath entered into glory, having thenceforth power and authority to reedem, purify, and glorify all those who come unto Him as a mediator between God and mankind.

"Such being our motives, we can no longer be silent concerning the seed of metals, but declare that it is contained in the ores of metals, as wheat is in the grain; and the sottish folly of alchemists has hindered them from adverting to this, so that they have always sought it in the vulgar metals, which are factitious and not a natural production, herein acting as foolishly as if a man should sow bread and expect corn from it, *or from an egg which is boiled hope to produce a chicken.* Nay, though the philosophers have said many times the vulgar metals are dead, not excepting gold, which passes the fire, they could never imagine a thing so simple as that the seed of metals was contained in their ores, where alone it ought to be expected; so bewildered is human ingenuity, when it leaves the beaten track of truth and Nature, to entangle itself in a multiplicity of finespun inventions.

"The searcher of Nature will rejoice greatly in this discovery, as grounded in reason and sound philosophy, but to fools it would be in vain, should even Wisdom herself cry out in the streets. Wherefore, leaving such persons to hug themselves in their own imaginary importance, we shall go on to observe that the ores of metals are our First Matter, or sperm, wherein the seed is contained, and the key of this art consists in a right dissolution of the ores into a water, which the philosophers call their mercury, or water of life, and an earthly substance, which they have denominated their sulphur. The first is called their woman, wife, Luna, and other names, signifying that it is the feminine quality in their seed; and the other they have denominated their man, husband, Sol, etc., to point out its masculine quality. In the separation and due conjunction of these with heat, and careful management, there is generated a noble offspring, which they have for its excellency called the quintessence or a subject wherein the four elements are so completely harmonized as to produce a fifth subsisting in the fire, without waste of substance, or diminution of its virtue, wherefore they have given it the titles of Salamander, Phoenix, and Son of the Sun.

"The true Sons of Science have always accounted the dissolution of metals as the master key to this art, and have been particular in giving directions concerning it, only keeping their readers in the dark as to the subject, whether ores, or factitious metals, were to be chosen: nay, when they say most to the purpose, then they make mention of metals rather than the ores, with an intention to perplex those whom they thought unworthy of the art. Thus, the author of the *Philosophical Duel*, or a dialogue between the stone, gold, and mercury, says:

"'By the omnipotent God, and on the salvation of my soul, I here declare to you earnest seekers, in pity to your earnest searching, the whole Philosophical Work, which is only taken from one subject and perfected in one thing. For we take this copper, and destroy its crude and gross body; we draw out its pure spirit, and after we have purified the earthy parts, we join them together, thus making a medicine of a poison.'

"It is remarkable that he avoids mentioning the ore, but calls his subject copper, which is what they call a metal of the vulgar, being indeed factitious, and not fit for the confection of our Stone, having lost its seminal quality in the fire; but in other respects it is the plainest discovery extant, and is accounted to be so by Sendivogious.

"Yet the reader is not to suppose that the ore of copper is to be chosen in consequence of that assertion, as preferable to others. No, the mercury, which is the metallic seed, is attainable from all, and is easier to be extracted from lead, which is confirmed by the true adepts, advising us to seek for the noble child where it lies in a despised form, shut up under the seal of Saturn; and, indeed, let it be supposed, for an illustration of this subject, that if any one would propose to make malt, he may effect his purpose in the other corns, but barley is generally chosen, because its germ is made to sprout by a less tedious process, which is to all intents and purposes what we want in the extraction of our mercury: neither are the proceedings unsimilar in both cases, if regard is had to the fixity of ores, and the ease with which barley gives forth its seminal virtue from the slight cohesion of its parts.

"Let the artist remark how a maltster manages his grain by wetting, to loosen the cohesion of its parts, and leaves the rest to Nature, knowing that she will soon furnish the necessary heat for his purpose, if he does not suffer it to escape by mismanagement in the laying of his heap too thin, or raising the fermentation too high by a contrary proceeding, as it is well known actual fire may be kindled from the fermentation of vegetable juices when crude; and ripe corn, under such treatment, would soon be fit for nothing but hogs, or the dunghill. Now the intention is to raise such a fermentation only as will draw out the vegetable mercury without spoiling it, either for the earth, if it was cast there to fructify, or the kiln, if it is to be fixed at that precise point, by exhaling the adventitious moisture, and thus preserving the whole strength of its seminal quality for the purposes of brewing, or making malt spirits.

"Suppose, then, an artist would extract a mineral mercury from the ores, and chooses lead ore for his subject. He can only assist Nature in the process by stirring up a central heat, which she includes in everything not already putrefied, as a root of its life, in which it is increased. The medium by which this central heat is put in motion is known to be putrefaction; but the ores of every kind are found to resist putrefaction in all known processes extant. They may, indeed, when they have been fluxed in the fire, contract a rust from the air, which is a gradual decomposition of their substance, but this is only the natural decay of a dead body, not the putrefaction of its sperm for the purposes of propagation; and we are sensible from the heat of furnaces which is required to flux ores, and the slowness of their decay when deprived of their seminal qualities, by fluxation, that a heat which would destroy the seed in vegetables may be necessary in the first stages of putrefaction for the ores, as they will bear a red fire without being fluxed or losing anything but their sulphureous and arsenical impurities; in short, a matter in itself as much extraneous to the seed of metals, as the chaff to the wheat: wherefore, a careful separation of these by roasting, or otherwise, is deservedly reckoned among the first operations for the putrefaction of ores, and the rather because that which has been calcined, by having its pores opened, is rendered attractive, both of the air and other menstruums proper for its decomposition.

"Let the artist, therefore, by fire and manual operation, separate the impure qualities from his subject, pounding, washing, and calcining, till no more blackness is communicated to his menstruum, for which pure rainwater is sufficient. It will be seen on every repetition of this process, that what fouls the water is extraneous and the ore yet exists in its individual metallic nature, except it is fluxed by a too intense heat, in which case it is no longer fit for our purpose; therefore, fresh ore is to be used.

"The matter being thus prepared, its central fire will be awakened, if it is treated properly, according to the process for extracting quicksilver from its ores, by keeping it in a close heat, which is continued without admission of the crude air, till the radical moisture is elevated in the form of a vapour, and again condensed into a metallic water, analogous to quicksilver. This is the true mercury of the Philosophers, and fit for all their operations in the Hermetic Art.

"The putrefaction of our subject being thus completed, it exists under two forms: the moisture which was extracted, and the residuum, being our Philosophical Earth and Water. The water contains its seminal virtue, and the earth is a proper receptacle, wherein it may fructify. Let the water, then, be separated and kept for use; calcine the earth, for an impurity adheres to it which can only be taken away by fire, and that, too, of the strongest degree: for here there is no danger of destroying the seminal quality, and our earth must be highly purified before it can ripen the seed. This is what Sendivogius means when he says: *Burn the sulphur till it becomes sulphur incombustible. Many lose in the preparation what is of most use in the art; for our mercury is acuated by the sulphur, else it would be of no use.* Let, therefore, the earthy part be well calcined, and return the mercury on the calcined earth; afterwards draw it off by distillation; then calcine, cohobate, and distil, repeating the process till the mercury is well acuated by the sulphur, and the sulphur is purified to a whiteness, and goes to a red, a sign of its complete purification, where you have the Philosophical Male and Female ready for conjunction. This must now be managed with judgment, as the noble child may be yet strangled in the birth; but all things are easy to an ingenious artist, who knows the proportion of mixture required and accommodates his operations to the intentions of Nature, for which purpose we shall faithfully conduct him according to our ability.

Of The Union Or Mystical Marriage In The Philosophical Process

"The seed and its earth being thus prepared nothing remains but a judicious conjunction of them together; for if too much moisture prevails, the philosophical egg may be burst before it can go through the heat necessary for its hatching. To speak without a figure, our subject must now be enclosed in a small glass vial, made strong enough to bear a due heat, which is to be raised gradually to the highest degree: the best form for this vessel being that of an oil flask, with a long neck; but these are much too thin in substance for this operation. In such a vessel the mixture is to be sealed hermetically, and digested so long till it is fixed into a dry concretion: but, if, as we observed, the moisture should predominate, there is great danger of the vessel bursting, with a vapour which cannot be concentered by the fixing quality in the matter. The intention is, nevertheless, to fix our subject in the heat, and so render its future destruction impossible.

"On the other hand, if the dry, fixing quality of the sulphur exceeds so as not to suffer an alternate resolution of its substance into vapors, and a re-manifestation of its fixing quality, by causing the whole to subside in the bottom of the vessel till the matter again liquefies and sublimes (which Ripley has well described), there is danger of the whole vitrifying; and thus you shall have only glass instead of the noble tincture. To avoid these two extremes it is very proper that the purified earth be reduced by manual operation to an impalpable fineness, and then its acuated mercury must be added, incorporating both together till the earth will imbibe no more. This operation will require time, with some degree of the artist's patience; for however the humidity may seem disproportionate; on letting it rest a while, a dryness on the surface of your matter will show that it is capable of imbibing more, so that the operation is to be repeated till it is finally saturated, which may be known from its bearing the air without any remarkable change of surface from dry to humid; or, on the contrary, if so, the conjunction is well made, which is further confirmed if a small portion be spread upon a thin plate of iron, heated till it gently flows like wax, casting forth the moisture with heat and again absorbing it when cold, so as to return to the former consistence; but if a clamminess ensues it is a sign you have exceeded in the quantity of humidity, which must be extracted by distilling again and repeating the process till it is right.

"Your sulphur and mercury being thus united, put them into a glass vial, before described, in such a quantity as to take up one-third of its contents, leaving two-thirds, including the neck, for the circulation of your matter. Secure the neck of your vial with a temporary luting at the first, and give a gentle heat, observing whether it sublimes and fixes alternately. If it easily sublimes and shows a disposition, at intervals, to subside at the bottom of the vessel, all is well conducted hitherto; for the moisture will first be predominant, which the sulphur can only perfectly absorb as the heat is increased for the perfect ripening of our Paradisiacal Fruit. Therefore, if it manifests a too early disposition for fixing, add more of the acuated mercury till Luna rises resplendent in her season; she will give place to the Sun in his turn. This would be the language of an adept on this occasion, only suggesting that the female quality in our prepared seed is first active, while the male is passive, and that it is afterwards passive while the male is active, such being the case in all vegetation; for every germ which is the first rudiments of a herb or tree, is predominant in moisture, and then only becomes fixed when it is fully concocted in the seed.

Of The Further Treatment And Ripening Of Our Seed

"This is deservedly called the Great Work of the Philosophers; and the artist having done his part hitherto, must seal up his glass hermetically, an operation which every maker of barometers knows how to perform.

"The glass is then to be put into a furnace with a proper nest contrived for its reception, so as to give a continual heat from the first to the fourth degree, and to afford the artist an opportunity, from time to time, of inspecting every change which his matter assumes during the process, without danger of damping the heat and putting a stop to its perfect circulation. A heat of the first degree is sufficient at the first, for some months, in which method much time may be lost by a young practitioner, till he knows how to handle his matter from experience; but then he is not so liable to be disappointed with the bursting of his vessel or the matter vitrifying.

"Thus you have arrived at the desired seed-time in our Philosophical Work, which, though it may appear in the artist's power to ripen, depends no less on the Divine blessing than the harvest, which a painful husbandman has not the presumption to expect otherwise than from God's beneficence.

"There are many requisites to entitle anyone to the possession of our philosophical harvest, and the true labourers in it have sought for such persons to whom they might communicate it, by evident testimony of the senses, after which they account the confection of our Stone an easy process, manageable by women and children; but without such a communication, there is a necessity that those who would undertake it are endowed by Nature with an ingenious mind, patient to observe and accurate to investigate her ordinary appearances which, from their commonness, are less noticed than such phenomena as are more curious though of less importance; yet these for the most part employ the precious time of those egregious triflers, the modern virtuosi. These smatterers in philosophy are in raptures upon the discovery of a shell or butterfly differently streaked from those of the same kind; and all the while water, air, earth, fire, with their continual changes and resolutions into one another, by the medium of our atmosphere, through the efficacy of the central and solar heat, are unstudied by these would-be philosophers; so that a sensible rustic has more real knowledge, in this respect, than a collector of natural rarities, and makes a much wiser use of what experience he has acquired.

Of The Further Process To The Ripening Of Our Noble Seed

"Supposing such dispositions in the artist as have been previously laid down, and the work well performed hitherto, for his direction herein we shall describe the changes which our subject undergoes during the second part of the process, commonly called the Great Work of the Philosophers.

"Our vessel being warily heated at the first for fear of its cracking, an ebullition of the contained matter is brought on, so that the moisture is alternately circulated in white fumes above, and condensed below, which may continue for a month or two, nay longer, increasing the heat gradually to another degree, as your matter discovers a disposition for fixing, by the vapour continuing at longer intervals condensed, and rising in a lesser quantity, of an ash colour, or other dark shades, which it will assume as a medium to perfect blackness, the first desirable stage in our harvest. Other colours may be exhibited in this part of the work without danger, if they pass transiently; but if a faint redness, like that of a corn poppy continues, the matter is in danger of vitrifying, either from an impatient urging of the fire, or the moisture not being sufficiently predominant. An ingenious artist can remedy this by opening his vessel and adding more of the acuated mercury, sealing it up as before; but a novice would do much better to prevent it by governing his fire according to the appearances of his matter, with judgment and patience, increasing it if the moisture manifests its predominancy too long, and slacking if the dry prevails, till such time as the vapours become dark; and after they have continued for some time at rest, a pellicle or film on the matter shows its disposition for fixing, retaining the vapour captive for some time, till it breaks through at different places on its surface (much like the bituminous substance of coal in a smoldering fire), with darker clouds, but quickly dissipated, and growing less in quantity, till the whole substance resembles molten pitch, or the aforesaid bituminous substance, bubbling less and less, resting in one entire black substance at the bottom of your glass. This is called the blackness of black, the head of the crow, etc., and is esteemed a desirable stage in our philosophical generation, being the perfect putrefaction of our seed, which will ere long show its vital principle by a glorious manifestation of Seminal Virtue.

A Further Description Of The Process

"When the putrefaction of our seed has been thus completed, the fire may be increased till glorious colours appear, which the Sons of Art have called *Cauda Pavonis*, or the Peacock's Tail. These colours come and go, as heat is administered approaching to the third degree, till all is of a beautiful green, and as it ripens assumes a perfect whiteness, which is the White Tincture, transmuting the inferior metals into silver, and very powerful as a medicine. But as the artist well knows it is capable of a higher concoction, he goes on increasing his fire, till it assumes a yellow, then an orange or citron colour and then boldly gives a heat of the fourth degree, till it acquires a redness like blood taken from a sound person, which is a manifest sign of its thorough concoction and fitness for the uses intended.

Of The Stone And Its Uses

"Having thus completed the operation, let the vessel cool, and on opening it you will perceive your matter to be fixed into a ponderous mass, thoroughly of a scarlet colour, which is easily reducible to powder by scraping, or otherwise, and in being heated in the fire flows like wax, without smoking, flaming, or loss of substance, returning when cold to its former fixity, heavier than gold, bulk for bulk, yet easy to be dissolved in any liquid, in which a few grains being taken its operation most wonderfully pervades the human body, to the extirpation of all disorders, prolonging life by its use to its utmost period; and hence it has obtained the appelation of "Panacea," or universal remedy. Therefore, be thankful to the Most High for the possession of such an inestimable jewel, and account the possession of it not as a result of your own ingenuity, but a gift bestowed, of God's mere bounty, for the relief of human infirmities, in which your neighbour ought to share jointly with you, without any grudging or sinister views, according to the charge delivered to the Apostles, "Freely have you received, freely communicate," remembering at the same time not to cast your pearls before swine; in a word to withhold the manifestations of Nature you are enabled to exhibit, by the possession of our Stone, from the vicious and unworthy.

"It is much to be lamented that the seekers of natural knowledge in this art propose, principally, the Science of Transmutation as their ultimate view, and overlooking the chief excellency of our Stone as a medicine. Notwithstanding this grovelling spirit, we shall commit the issue to His Providence, and declare the Transmutation (which, indeed, the philosophers do) openly, after which we shall describe the further circulation of our Stone for an increase of its virtues, and then make an end of our treatise.

"When the artist would transmute any metal—for instance, lead—let a quantity be melted in a clean crucible, to which let a few grains of gold in filings be cast; and when the whole is melted, let him have in readiness a little of the powder, which will easily scrape off from his "stone," the quantity inconsiderable, and cast it on the metal while in fusion. Immediately there will arise a thick fume, which carries off with it the impurities contained in the lead, with a crackling noise, and leaves the substance of the lead transmuted into most pure gold, without any kind of sophistication; the small quantity of gold added, previous to projection, serves only as a medium to facilitate the transmutation, and the quantity of your tincture is best ascertained by experience, as its virtue is proportioned to the number of circulations you have given after the first has been completed.

"For instance: when you have finished the stone, dissolve it in our mercury again, wherein you have previously dissolved a few grains of pure gold. This operation is done without trouble, both substances readily liquefying. Put it into your vessel, as before, and go through the process. There is no danger in the management, but breaking your vessel; and every time it is thus treated its virtues are increased, in a ratio of ten to one hundred, a thousand, ten thousand, etc., both in medicinal and transmuting qualities; so that a small quantity may suffice for the purposes of an artist during the remaining term of his life."

Basil Valentine, the German Benedictine monk, whose name deserves great respect in Alchemy, has given posterity precious pearls of wisdom when he states in his famous work, *Currus Triumphalis Antimonii (Triumphal Chariot of Antimony):*

"You should know that all things contain operative and vital spirits which derive their substance and nourishment from their bodies; nor are the elements themselves without these spirits, whether good or evil. Men and animals have within them an operative and vitalizing spirit, and if it forsakes them, nothing but a dead body is left. Herbs and trees have spirits of health, else no art could turn them to medicinal uses. In the same way minerals and metals possess vitalizing spirits which constitute their whole strength and goodness; for what has no spirit has no life, or vitalizing power."

Again, he says so plainly what alchemical students should keep in mind when working in their laboratories and trying to fix that elusive Mercury of the minerals:

"No animal or vegetable contains anything that can avail to fix Mercury; the attempt to do this has always ended in failure, because none of these substances have a metallic nature. Mercury is both inwardly and outwardly pure fire: therefore no fire can destroy it, no fire can change its essence; it flees from the fire, and resolves itself into an incombustible oil spiritually; but when it is once fixed, no cunning of man can volatilize it again. Then everything can by art be made of it that can be produced from gold, because after its coagulation it perfectly resembles gold, seeing that it has grown from the same root, and sprung from exactly the same branch as that precious metal."

(The great question which vexes all the students of our Art, 'What is our Mercury?' is here clearly and lucidly answered. Attend carefully to all that Basilius says. Any light that I could add to his brightness would be darkness indeed.—This annotation is from the commentary of Theodore Kerkringius in the Latin version of 1685, published in Amsterdam.)

"Let me tell you then that all metals and minerals grow in the same way from the same root, and that thus all metals have a common origin. This first principle is a mere vapour extracted from the elementary earth through the heavenly planets and, as it were, divided by the sidereal distillation of the Macrocosmos. This sidereal hot infusion, descending from on high into those things which are below, with the aero-sulphureous property, so acts and works as to engraft on them in a spiritual and invisible manner a certain strength and virtue. This vapour afterwards resolves itself in the earth into a kind of water, and out of this mineral water all metals are generated and perfected. The mineral vapour becomes this or that metal according as one or the other of the three first principles predominates, i.e., according as they have much or little mercury, sulphur, or salt, or an unequal mixture or their weights. Hence, some metals are fixed; some are permanent and unchangeable; some are volatile and variable, as you may see in gold, silver, copper iron, tin, and lead.

"Besides these metals, other minerals are generated from these three principles; according to the proportion of the ingredients, we have vitriol, antimony, marcasite, electrum, and many other minerals."

In an exceedingly rare volume of treatises, *The Hermetic Museum*, published in Frankfort in 1678, we find in *The Open Entrance to the Closed Palace of the King* (by "An Anonymous Sage and Lover of Truth," whom we discover to be Eirenaeus Philalethes) the following under the heading, "Of the Difficulty and Length of the First Operation."

"Some alchemists fancy that the work from beginning to end is a mere idle entertainment; but those who make it so will reap what they have sown—viz., nothing. We know that next to the Divine Blessing, and the discovery of the proper foundation, nothing is so important as unwearied industry and perseverance in this First Operation. It is no wonder, then, that so many students of this Art are reduced to beggary; they are afraid of work, and look upon our Art as mere sport for their leisure moments. For no labour is more tedious than that which the preparatory part of our enterprise demands. Morienus earnestly entreats the King to consider this fact, and says that many Sages have complained of the tedium of our work. 'To render a chaotic mass orderly,' says the Poet, 'is matter of much time and labour'—and the noble author of the Hermetical Arcanum describes it as Herculean task. There are so many impurities clinging to our first substance, and a most powerful intermediate agent is required for the purpose of eliciting from our polluted menstruum the Royal Diadem. But when you have once prepared your Mercury,* the most formidable part of your task

---

* *"On the Sulphur which is in the Mercury of the Sages.* It is a marvelous fact that our Mercury contains *active* Sulphur, and yet preserves the form and all the properties of Mercury. Hence it is necessary that a form be introduced

is accomplished, and you may indulge in that rest which is sweeter than any work, as the Sage says."

"There are those who think that this Art was first discovered by Solomon, or rather imparted to him by Divine Revelation. But though there is no reason for doubting that so wise and profoundly learned a sovereign was acquainted with our Art, yet we happen to know that he was not the first to acquire the knowledge. It was possessed by Hermes, the Egyptian, and some other Sages before him; and we may suppose that they first sought a simple exaltation of imperfect metals into regal perfection, and that it was at first their endeavour to develop Mercury, which is most like to gold in its weight and properties, into perfect gold. This, however, no degree of ingenuity could effect by any fire, and the truth gradually broke on their minds that an internal heat was required as well as an external one. So they rejected aqua fortis and all corrosive solvents, after long experiments with the same — also all salts, except that kind which is the first substance of all salts, which dissolves all metals and coagulates Mercury, but not without violence, whence that kind of agent is again separated entire, both in weight and virtue, from the things it is applied to. They saw that the digestion of Mercury was prevented by certain aqueous crudities and earthy dross; and that the *radical*

---

therein by our preparation, which form is a metallic sulphur. This Sulphur is the inward fire which causes the putrefaction of the composite Sun. This sulphureous fire is the spiritual seed which our Virgin (still remaining immaculate) has conceived. For an uncorrupted virginity admits of a spiritual love, as experience and authority affirm. The two (the passive and the active principle) combined we call our Hermaphrodite. When joined to the Sun, it softens, liquefies, and dissolves it with a gentle heat. By means of the same fire it coagulates itself; and by its coagulation produces the Sun. Our pure and homogeneous Mercury having conceived inward Sulphur (through our Art), coagulates itself under the influence of gentle outward heat, like the cream of milk—a subtle earth floating on the water. When it is united to the Sun, it is not only not coagulated, but the composite substance becomes softer day by day; the bodies are almost dissolved, and the spirits begin to be coagulated, with a black color and a most fetid smell. Hence it appears that this spiritual metallic Sulphur is in truth the *moving principle in our Art;* it is really volatile or unmatured gold, and by proper digestion is changed into that metal. If joined to perfect gold, it is not coagulated but dissolves the corporal gold and remains with it, having dissolved, under one form, although before the perfect union death must precede, that so they may be united after death, not simply in a perfect unity, but in a thousand times more than perfect perfection."

nature of these impurities rendered their elimination impossible, except by the complete inversion of the whole compound. They knew that Mercury would become fixed if it could be freed from their defiling presence—as it contains fermenting sulphur, which is only hindered by these impurities from coagulating the whole mercurial body. At length they discovered that Mercury, in the bowels of the earth, was intended to become a metal, and that the process of development was only stopped by the impurities with which it had become tainted. They found that that which should be active in Mercury was passive; and that its infirmity could not be remedied by any means, except the introduction of some kindred principle from without. Such a principle they discovered in metallic sulphur, which stirred up the passive sulphur in the Mercury, and by allying itself with it, expelled the aforesaid impurities. But in seeking to accomplish this practically, they were met by another great difficulty. In order that this sulphur might be effectual in purifying the Mercury, it was indispensable that it should itself be pure.

"All their efforts to purify it, however, were doomed to failure. At length they bethought them that it might possibly be found somewhere in nature in a purified condition—and their search was crowned with success. They sought active sulphur in a pure state, and found it cunningly concealed in the House of the Ram.* This sulphur mingled most eagerly with the offspring of Saturn, and the desired effect was speedily produced—after the malignant venom of the "air" of Mercury had been tempered (as already set forth at some length) by the doves of Venus. Then life was joined to life by means of the liquid; the dry was moistened; the passive was stirred into action by the active; the dead was revived by the living. The heavens were indeed temporarily clouded over, but after a copious downpour of rain, serenity was restored. Mercury emerged in a hermaphroditic state. Then they placed it in the fire; in no long time they succeeded in coagulating it, and in its coagulation they found the Sun and the Moon in a most pure state. Then they considered that, before its coagulation, this Mercury was not a metal, since, on being vola-

---

* Here is the key. What planet rules Aries? What metal does this planet rule? Saturn rules what metal? Where can the sulphur be extracted from the "unripe" Mercury. Now you have the secret unfolded.

tilised, it left no residue at the bottom of the distilling vessel; hence they called it unmatured gold and their living (or quick) silver. It also occurred to them that if gold were sown, as it were, in the soil of its own first substance, its excellence would probably be enhanced, and when they placed gold therein, the fixed was volatilised, the hard softened, the coagulated dissolved, to the amazement of Nature herself. For this reason they wedded these two to each other, put them in a still over the fire, and for many days regulated the heat in accordance with the requirements of Nature. Thus the dead was revived, the body decayed, and a glorified spirit rose from the grave; the soul was exalted into the quintessence—the Universal Medicine for animals, vegetables, and minerals."

At first it will seem that the quotation above is a book sealed seven times seven. As is the case with all alchemystical literature, a prolonged contemplation will eventually reveal its true meaning in the plainest manner imaginable. What had formerly seemed to be a jargon of gibberish and nonsense will gradually reveal itself in a very simple form.

If we penetrate even further, we will come to know one of the valiant defenders of the Hermetic Brethren. He is none other than the mystery figure, Michael Sendivogius.

The name, Michael Sendivogius, whose name was concealed in his anagram, "Divi Leschi genus amo" ("I love the divine race of Leschi"), will have frequently confronted the reader of alchemystical literature. In his *The New Chemical Light,* which he says is "drawn from the fountain of nature *and of manual* experience," he states in part:

"Upon all genuine Seekers of the great Chemical Art, or Sons of Hermes, the Author implores the Divine Blessing and Salvation.

"When I considered in my mind the great number of deceitful books and forged Alchemistic 'receipts,' which have been put in circulation by heartless impostors, though they do not contain even a spark of truth—and how many persons have been and are still daily led astray by them?—it occurred to me that I could not do better than communicate the Talent committed to me by the Father of Lights to the Sons and Heirs of Knowledge. I also wish to let posterity see that in our own age, as well as in ancient times, this singularly gracious philosophical Blessing has not been denied to a few favoured men. For certain reasons I do not think it advisable to publish my name; chiefly, because I do not seek for praise for myself, but am only anxious to assist the lovers of philosophy. The vainglorious desire for fame I leave to those who are content to seem what they, in reality, are not. The facts and deductions which I have here briefly set down are transcribed from that manual—experience, graciously bestowed upon me by the Most High; and my object is to enable those who have laid a sound foundation in the elementary part of this most noble Art, to advance to a more satisfying fullness of knowledge, and to put them on their guard against those depraved 'vendors of smoke' who delight in fraud and imposition. Our science is not a dream, as the vulgar crowd imagines, or the empty invention of idle men, as the foolish suppose. It is the very truth of philosophy itself, which the voice of conscience and of love bid me to conceal no longer.

"In these wicked days, indeed, when virtue and vice are accounted alike, the ingratitude and unbelief of men keep our Art from appearing openly before the public gaze. Yet this glorious truth is even now capable of being apprehended by learned and unlearned persons of virtuous lives, and there are many persons of all nations now living who have beheld Diana unveiled. But as many, either from ignorance or from a desire to conceal their knowledge, are daily teaching and inducing others to believe that the soul of gold can be extracted, and then imparted to other substances; and thereby entice numbers to incur great waste of time, labour, and money; let the sons of Hermes know for certain that the extracting of the essence of gold is a mere fond delusion, as those who persist in it will be taught to their cost by experience, the only arbitress from whose judgment seat there is no appeal. If, on the other hand, a person is able to transmute the smallest piece of metal (with or without gain) into genuine gold or silver which abides all the usual tests, he may justly be said to have opened the gates of Nature, and cleared the way for profounder and more advanced study.

"It is with this object that I dedicate the following pages, which embody the results of my experience, to the sons of knowledge, that by a careful study of the working of Nature they may be enabled to lift the veil, and enter her inmost sanctuary. To this final goal of our sacred philosophy they must travel by the royal road which Nature herself has marked out for them. Let me therefore admonish the gentle reader that my meaning is to be apprehended not so much from the outward husk of my words, as from the inward spirit of Nature. If this warning is neglected, he may spend his time, labour, and money in vain. Let him consider that this mystery is for wise men, and not for fools. The inward meaning of our philosophy will be unintelligible to vainglorious boasters, to conceited mockers, and to men who smother the clamorous voice of conscience with the insolence of a wicked life; as also to those ignorant persons who have fondly staked their happiness on albafactions and rubefactions and other equally senseless methods. The right understanding of our Art is by the gift of God, or by the ocular demonstration of a teacher, and can be attained only by the diligent, humble search and prayerful dependence on the Giver of all good things; now, God rejects those who hate Him and scorn knowledge. In conclusion, I would earnestly ask the sons of knowledge to accept this book in the spirit in which it was written; and when the HIDDEN has become MANIFEST to them, and the inner gates of secret knowledge are flung open, not to reveal this mystery to any unworthy person; also to remember their duty towards their suffering and distressed neighbors, to avoid any ostentatious display of their power; and above all, to render to God, the Three in One, sincere and grateful thanks with their lips, in the silence of their hearts, and by refraining from any abuse of the gift.

"As after the completion of the preface, it was found that it did not cover the whole of the space allotted to it, I have at the publisher's request, there set down 'the last will and testament of Arnold Villanovanus,' which I once turned into Latin verse. I am conscious that the style of my versification is wanting in neatness and elegance; but this defect was partly caused by the necessity of adhering strictly and faithfully to the author's meaning.

"It is said that Arnold de Villanova, a man who was a credit to his race, signified his last will in the following words: 'It has its birth in the earth, its strength it doth acquire in the fire, and there becomes the true Stone of the ancient Sages. Let it be nourished for twice six hours with a clear liquid until its limbs begin to expand and grow apace. Then let it be placed in a dry and moderately warm spot for another period of twelve hours, until it has purged itself by giving out a thick steam or vapour, and becomes solid and hard within. The *Virgin's Milk* that is expressed from the better part of the Stone is then preserved in a carefully closed oval-shaped distilling vessel of glass, and is day by day wondrously changed by the quickening fire, until all the different colors resolve themselves into a fixed, gentle splendor of a white radiance which soon under the continued genial influence of the fire, changes to a glorious purple the outward and visible sign of the final perfection of your work.'

"Many Sages, scholars, and learned men have in all ages and (according to Hermes) even so early as the days before the Flood, written much concerning the preparation of the Philosopher's Stone; and if their books could be understood without a knowledge of the living processes of Nature, one might almost say that they are calculated to supersede the study of the real world around us. But though they never departed from the simple ways of Nature they have something to teach us, which we in these more sophisticated times, still need to learn, because we have applied ourselves to what are regarded as the more advanced branches of knowledge, and despise the study of so 'simple' a thing as natural Generation. Hence, we pay more heed to impossible things than to those objects which are broadly exhibited before our very eyes; we excel more in subtle speculations than in a sober study of Nature, and of the meaning of the Sages. It is one of the most remarkable features of human nature that we neglect those things which seem familiar, and are eager for new and strange information. The workman who has attained the highest degree of excellence in his Art, neglects it, and applies himself to something else, or else, abuses his knowledge. Our longing for an increase of knowledge urges us ever onward toward some final goal, in which we imagine that we shall find full rest and satisfaction, like the ant, which is not endowed with wings till the last days of its life. In our time, the Philosophical Art has become a very subtle matter; it is the craft of the goldsmith compared with that of the humble workman who exercises his calling at the forge. We have made such mighty strides in advance that if the ancient Masters of our science, Hermes and Geber and Raymond Lullius, were to rise from the dead, they would be treated by our modern Alchemists, not as Sages, but as only humble learners. They would seem very poor scholars in our modern lore of futile distillations, circulations, calcinations, and in all the other countless operations wherewith modern research has so famously enriched our Art. In all these respects, our learning is vastly superior to theirs. Only one thing is unfortunately wanting to us which they possessed, namely, the knack they had of actually preparing the Philosopher's Stone. Perhaps, then, their simple methods were after all the best; and it is on this supposition that I desire, in this volume, to teach you to understand Nature, so that our vain imaginations may not misdirect us in the true and simple way. Nature, then, is one, true, simple, self-contained, created by God and informed with a certain universal spirit. Its end and origin are God. Its unity is also found in God, because God made all things. Nature is the one source of all things: nor is anything in the world outside Nature, or contrary to Nature. Nature is divided into four 'places' in which she brings forth all things that appear and that are in the shade; and according to the good or bad quality of the 'place' she brings forth good or bad things. There are only four qualities which are in all things and yet do not agree among themselves, as one is always striving to obtain the mastery over the rest. Nature is not visible, though she acts visibly; she is a volatile spirit who manifests herself in material shapes, and her existence is in the Will of God. It is most important for us to know her 'places,' and those which are most in harmony, and most closely allied, in order that we may join things together according to Nature, and not attempt to confound vegetables with animals, or animals with metals. Everything should be made to act on that which is like to it—and then Nature will perform her duty.

"Students of Nature should be such as is Nature herself—true, simple, patient, constant, and so on; above all, they should fear God and love their neighbors. They should always be ready to learn from Nature, and to be guided by her methods, ascertaining by visible and sensible examples whether that which they propose to perform is in accordance with her possibilities. If we would reproduce something already accomplished by Nature, we must follow her, but if we would improve on her performance, we must know in and by what it is ameliorated. For instance, if we desire to impart to a metal greater excellence than Nature has given to it, we must take the *metallic* substance both in its male and female varieties, else all our efforts will be in vain. It is as impossible to produce a metal out of a plant as to make a tree out of a dog or any other animal.

"I have already said that Nature is one, true, and consistent, and that she is known by her products, such as trees, herbs, etc. I have also described the qualifications of a student of Nature. Now I will say a few words about the operation of Nature.

"As Nature has her being in the Will of God, so her will or seed is in the Elements. She is one and produces different things, but only through the mediate instrumentality of seed. For Nature performs whatsoever the sperm requires of her and is, as it were, only the instrument of some artisan. The seed, if anything, is more useful to the artist than Nature herself; for Nature without seed is what a goldsmith is without silver and gold, or a husbandman without seed-corn. Wherever there is seed, Nature will work through it, whether it be good or bad. Nature works on 'seed' as God works on the free will of man. Truly it is a great marvel to behold Nature obeying the seed, not because she is forced to do so, but of her own will. In like manner God permits man to do what he pleases, not because He is constrained, but of His good and free bounty. The seed, then, is the elixir of anything or its quintessence, or its most perfect digestion or decoction or, again, the Balm of Sulphur which is the same as the radical moisture in metals. We might say much more about this seed, but can only mention those facts which are of importance to our Art. The four elements produce seed, through the will of God and the imagination of Nature; and as the seed of the male animal has its center or storing place in the kidneys, so the four elements by their continual action project a constant supply of seed to the center of the earth, where it is digested, and whence it proceeds again in generative motions. Now the center of the earth is a certain void place wherein nothing is at rest; and upon the margin or circumference of this center the four elements project their qualities. As the male seed is emitted into the womb of the female, where only so much as is needed is retained while the rest is driven out again, so the magnetic force of our earth-center attracts to itself as much as is needed of the cognate seminal substance, while that which cannot be used for vital generation is thrust forth in the shape of stones and other rubbish. This is the fountainhead of all things terrestrial.

"Let us illustrate the matter by supposing a glass of water to be

WISDOM OF THE SAGES

set in the middle of a table, round the margin of which are placed little heaps of salt and of powders of different colors. If the water be poured out, it will run all over the table in divergent rivulets, and will become salt where it touches the salt, red where it dissolves the red powder, and so on. The water does not change the 'places,' but the several places differentiate the water. In the same way, the seed which is the product of the four elements is projected in all directions from the earth-center, and produces different things according to the quality of the different places. Thus, while the seed of all things is one, it is made to generate a great variety of things, just as the seed of man might produce a man if projected into the womb of a female of his own species, or a monstruous variety of abortions, if projected into the wombs of different female animals. So long as Nature's seed remains in the center, it can indifferently produce a tree or a metal, a herb or a stone and, in like manner, according to the purity of the place, it will produce what is less or more pure. But how do the elements generate the sperm or seed? There are four elements, two heavy and two light, two dry and two moist, but one driest and one moistest of all; and these are male and female. By God's Will each of these is constantly striving to produce things like to itself in its own sphere. Moreover, they are constantly acting on one another, and the subtle essences of all are combined in the center, where they are well mixed and sent forth again by Archeus, the servant of Nature, as is more fully set forth in the Epilogue of these twelve Treatises.

"The first matter of metals is twofold, and one without the other cannot create a metal. The first and principal substance is the moisture of air mingled with warmth. This substance the Sages have called Mercury, and in the philosophical sea it is governed by the rays of the Sun and the Moon. The second substance is the dry heat of the earth, which is called Sulphur. But as this substance has always been kept a great mystery, let us declare it more fully, and especially its weight, ignorance of which mars the whole work. The right substance, if the quantity of it which is taken be wrong, can produce nothing but an abortion. There are some who take the entire body for their matter, that is, for their seed or sperm; others take only a part of it: both are on the wrong track. If anyone, for instance, were to attempt the creation of a man out of a man's hand and a woman's foot, he would fail. For there is in every body a central atom, or vital point of the seed (its 1/8200 part), even in a grain of wheat. Neither the body nor the grain is *all* seed, but every body has a small seminal spark, which the other parts protect from all excess of heat and cold.

"If you have ears and eyes treasure up this fact, and be on your guard against those who would use the whole grain as seed, and those who strive to produce a highly rarefied metallic substance by the vain solution and mixture of different metals. For even the purest metals contain a certain element of impurity, while in the inferior the proportion is greater. You will have all you want if you find the point of Nature which you must not, however, look for in the vulgar metals; it is not to be found therein, for all these and common gold more especially, are dead. But the metals which we advise you to take are living and have vital spirits. Fire is the life of metals while they are still in their ore, and the fire of smelting is their death. But the first matter of metals is a certain moisture mixed with warm air. Its appearance is that of oily water adhering to all pure and impure things; yet in some places it is found more abundantly than in others, because the earth is more open and porous in one place than in another, and has a greater magnetic force.

"When it becomes manifest, it is clothed in a certain vesture, especially in places where it has nothing to cling to. It is known by the fact that it is composed of three principles but, as a metallic substance, it is only one without any visible sign of conjunction, except that which may be called its vesture or shadow, namely, sulphur, etc."

Now to quote Paracelsus, that genius of the early sixteenth century, who long before Hahnemann, the supposed founder of homeopathy, and Prof. Liebig, the famous German chemist (both of whom are quoted in another chapter), explained why trituration is essential in the administering of medications. As will be seen from the following, not only Hahnemann, but Paracelsus before him, also taught the principles of homeopathy to the masses:

"We speak also in like manner concerning the magisteries of herbs which, indeed, are so efficacious that *half an ounce* of them operates more than a *hundred ounces* of their body, because scarcely the hundredth part is Quintessence. So, then, the quantity thereof being so very small, a greater mass of it has to be used and administered, which is not required in the case of magisteries; for in these the whole quantity of the herbs is reduced into a magistery, which is not then on account of its artificial character, to be judged inferior to the true extracted Quintessence itself. One part of this being exhibited is of more avail than a hundred parts of a similar body, for this reason, because the magisteries are prepared and rendered acute to the highest degree, and are brought to a quality equal to a Quintessence in which magistery all the virtues and powers of the body are present, and from these its own helping power arises to it. For in them the penetrability and the power of the whole body exist from the mixture that is made with it." *(The Archidoxies,* Book VI)

In conclusion, may the wisdom that speaks out of Paracelsus remind us always that "Alchemy indeed brings forth many excellent and sublime arcana to the light, which have been accidentally discovered rather than sought for. Wherefore let Alchemy be great and venerable in the sight of everyone, for many arcana are in tartar, in juniper, in melissa, in tincture, in vitriol, in salt, in alum, in Luna and in Sol." *(De Caducis,* Par. IV)

CONCLUSION

The curious and extraordinary aura surrounding the mystical alchemists is overwhelming even to the casual reader of their works. Understanding these immensely great human minds accelerates the individual consciousness to such tremendous heights that often, if only subconsciously, the boundaries of mundane science are surpassed. Even today, in our rapidly evolving, so-called modern times, when newer systems of both a physical and psychological nature are continuously confronting the inquiring minds of searchers for cosmic realization, it is astounding to find that these great philosophers, doctors of medicine, and alchemists are still too far advanced even for our "enlightened" age. Even individuals who have been only partly initiated into certain cosmic secrets and who—after due preparation—have found the keys to unlock the purposely strange and allegorically concealed formulas of the great alchemists, have been awed by the immense possibilities opening before them. Prior to this, such potentialities would have been considered utter impossibilities.

If alchemists, then, are such truly great scientists and if their teachings are of such tremendous benefit to mankind, why, the reader will complain, have they concealed their wisdom behind allegorical symbols that only confuse and mislead a searching mind? To ask such a question is not only natural, it is even justified. There is an answer to be given, and a very simple one: "It had to be done." "But why?" the reader will protest. "Why all this secrecy? Why haven't the alchemists written plainly, so that everyone reading these works will understand and benefit by them?"

What follows is a feeble attempt to vindicate the works of these great personages in the eyes of the searching, and so far unsuccessful, student. In reality, they need no vindication, for their names deserve to be pronounced with deepest reverence as divinely ordained cosmic ambassadors. To be specific, for instance, Paracelsus did not teach

100

new laws. He merely promulgated more openly and in a newer version what others before him had known and kept secret. He added to and perfected different methods for obtaining in simpler forms and in various ways, results that mundane science, as we understand it, cannot accomplish at present.

It is here that one of the secrets is to be found. *At present* mundane science cannot accomplish it, yet mundane science is of arcane birth. It represents the cosmic permission for segments of the arcane to become mundane. From time to time, more of the arcane wisdom, kept hidden from the profane, will be permitted to reach the consciousness of individuals in greater proportions. In the future, as in the past, it will do so through preordained channels. Evidence of this is apparent to the student of recorded history. Many discoveries that are common knowledge today were once the well guarded secrets of medieval alchemists. At one time, corrosive waters such as nitric acid (NHO_3) represented secret knowledge. Today we may purchase them for a few cents and put them to many common uses. However, we also find divine laws being employed by men for selfish purposes, and we must bear in mind that these laws work equally well in the hands of those unfortunate souls who place their egoism above the welfare of mankind. Laws do not operate successfully only in the hands of the good or the righteous, as we have seen to our cost in the annals of recorded history. Because of this, many laws known to the great alchemists were—and still are—kept concealed. Individual progress cannot be measured on a common scale. Inherent powers may be activated for various uses, producing results of different proportions, and yet they emanate from the same fundamental source or identical law. The arcane force creating heat in a terrestrial, visible fire is a manifestation of the same law that produces heat in an electric arc hot enough to melt metals. Once the workings of this law have been revealed and become the property of the individual, they may be used for either constructive or destructive purposes. The evolution of the human intellect depends on the cosmic permission for cosmic consciousness to penetrate and activate the functions of the brain, allowing always for the individual's free will and willingness to function as an agent of that consciousness. If Paracelsus and other alchemists, through cosmic permission and karma, were permitted to have revealed to them profound cosmic laws still generally unknown to the masses, then, instead of ridiculing these men, attempts should be made to unlock the mysteries of their work, and incorporate them for the beneficial use of mankind. This can be done. Herein lies another apparent secret.

Those who have demonstrated some of the teachings and formulas of Paracelsus know of it, but keep profound silence about their findings, as they are of such immense scope. If available as common knowledge, it would produce more good than most people could possibly stand without also doing undue harm. This statement may sound like the product of a sinister mind. But this is why alchemists concealed their findings. The transmutation of base metals into precious ones may be cited as an exemplary case. Mundane science has, with complicated physical processes, produced very small yet encouraging results. However, the cost is so enormous that the process is unprofitable at present. Alchemically, it may be accomplished by means of a comparatively simple process, presenting unlimited possibilities. How is this possible?[1] By knowing the secret.

What would be the natural result if a child had easy access to nitric acid even though he had been warned of its inherent poisonous qualities? He would either be afraid and shun it entirely, having before his eyes a mental picture of physical agony or even death; or curiosity would get the better of him to the extent that he would find out if the substance would do what is claimed of it. The results, of course, would depend upon the inherent intellect, even in a child. And results must eventually become evident. However, immaturity is not limited to the very young. Even today, all things are not for the *use* of everyone, although they were created for the benefit of all. It is for this reason that alchemists have had to conceal arcane knowledge. It illustrates, also, why their disciples refrain from revealing

---

[1] The common Norwegian rat, if permitted to multiply without restriction, would cover the earth in a relatively short time, making it theoretically impossible for humans to exist. The majority of men do not know how this law functions. Nevertheless, it functions irrespective of their ignorance as to why this law prevents the spread of rodents in such proportions, even though it is *theoretically* possible. It is under the operation of the same law that Alchemy is reserved for only a few. Eventually, the individual will master those laws which are now secret. But first man must attain to greater spiritual heights in order to comprehend, understand, and at last master himself.

such knowledge to everyone. It is because the parent *loves* the child, that he withholds certain knowledge until the child is prepared to receive it. In like manner, it is because the custodians of ageless wisdom love mankind that they must withhold certain portions of their knowledge until the student is prepared to receive it.

Mankind as a whole, at present, is not ready to receive this knowledge fully. In spite of the relatively high degree of civilization we have reached, mankind in its totality has not advanced very far. Its educational forces are being used deliberately for disruptive, not constructive, purposes. Wanton slaughter and annihilation are being perpetrated even by men who possess a belief in and knowledge of divine laws. Yet they clamor to learn greater and more sublime laws, while tragically demonstrating their inability to adhere to and master the lesser ones. What price ignorance! When we review the record of man's thoughtless abuse of the powers his knowledge of cosmic law has given him, we begin to understand the selective eye and secretive ways of the early alchemists. We can appreciate as never before the wisdom of their ancient maxim, still operative today, that only when the pupil is ready will the master appear. Certainly, Paracelsus was one of those masters, helping the student on the path through his exceedingly advanced teachings and postulates. Fortunately, however, only the initiated will be able to comprehend.

Emphasis is placed on the *initiated*. For those standing outside the realm of Alchemy, it is impossible to convey any proof. It is for this reason that true alchemists, from remotest times to the present day, have worked unknown, sometimes even to their own families. If one realizes that—on the surface at least—alchemical laboratory practice does not appear to differ from conventional chemical experimentation, it is not difficult to understand how alchemists in the past and in the present have been able to escape detection while still achieving valid alchemical accomplishments.

Alchemists labor primarily for the benefit of mankind. To concoct potent medicines from herbs and metals in order to heal the sick and restore normal body functions, is one of their prime activities. Nature, with its diverse herbs, roots, barks, minerals, and metals, is their true doctor. Alchemists act only as instruments. It is contrary to their character to offer Aesculapian sacrifices on the altar of ignorance, nor do they consider it wise to purposely adorn themselves with divinely revealed cosmic knowledge. They realize their own impotence in this great universe, and scrupulously exercise modesty and benevolence to the fullest degree. Many people think of alchemists as strange, mysterious individuals, half crazy, if not completely insane, who belong more properly to the Dark Ages. To mention that true alchemists are living and working today sounds, to most people, like a fable from *1001 Nights*. But the remarkable fact remains that even to this day, unknown to the world at large, alchemists continue to practice their art and science, faithful to a centuries-old tradition. More often than not, those apparent miracles that happen here and there are the results of the deeds of these unselfish men and women. In most cases, the identity of the benefactor remains unknown even to those who have benefitted. Puzzling as these statements may appear to be, the evidence cannot long be ignored by the medical profession. After all the scoffers have finished explaining away what they do not understand, the evidence for these miracles, as they have been termed, still remains. Many of the greatest practitioners of Alchemy, following a tradition of service to mankind, have concealed themselves behind mysterious pseudonyms or chosen the cloak of total anonymity. The dust of history, by their own choosing, has covered their individual personalities. But the solid record of their achievement remains, to baffle—and to challenge—the modern scientific mind.

The Difference Between Chemistry and Alchemy

How can a dividing line be drawn between chemistry and Alchemy? This question has often been asked. If chemistry is an outgrowth of medieval Alchemy, how can anything of benefit still remain in Alchemy? When the tincture of an herb has been extracted, only impotent leaves are left. The strength has been withdrawn. If this be true of Alchemy, then only a crude historical husk remains, and the essence, during the intervening centuries, has been extracted by modern chemistry. But with Alchemy, this is not so. We may compare it to a teacher who gives his knowledge to his pupils, and they again in turn to others. Although this knowledge may be worked with, the teacher has lost nothing by giving freely to others. Not only does he retain the knowledge he has given away, but other, untold knowledge remains within him, which he may convey to others whenever he sees fit. Much knowledge of the ancient alchemists that was formerly secret has become public property and been seized upon by others who proceeded to build various hypotheses upon it, out of which newer results developed. But not all alchemical knowledge has become public property. Much more yet remains to be expounded in university laboratories. It is here that the real controversy begins. To summarize the difference between Alchemy and present-day chemistry:

1. No one can accomplish anything alchemically in the laboratory without the Philosopher's Mercury, so-called. But this is not common metallic mercury or quicksilver.

2. The tincture (Philosopher's Mercury) including its Sulphur and the feces are to be first separated and then united again by proper processes.

There seems to be a tendency to go over the above statements too casually, not recognizing the importance of Mercury. This Philosopher's Mercury has been the troublemaker for centuries. Scientists, and by far the overwhelming majority of them, complain that it does not exist. It has not been discovered, they claim, nor can it be. And there they let the matter rest. Tampering with metallic mercury has brought about some results. Mercury bichloride and similar mercurial medications have been developed but, due to mercury's great venomous properties, only limited success has been obtained. Another striking difference is that any poison can be removed alchemically from any herb or metal and its healing and curing properties set free. This represents another stumbling block on the road of chemistry and medical science. If only poisons could be eliminated! Very seldom is a curative agent found that has not some poisonous substances adhering to it. To remove the venomous qualities, and to set free the curative agents, represents a heroic struggle that science, thus far, has not conquered.

"For humanity's sake," the public will exclaim, "for all the miseries existing in the world today, why don't the alchemists reveal their secrets? Why have people suffered and died in agony when there is help to be had?" It is this cry of humanity that pains the true alchemist most. Here the temptation to transgress the alchemist's oath is great indeed. Truly, the sorrows of mankind appear to afford well-founded, humanitarian reasons for overstepping the bounds of secrecy. And yet, as we stated on previous pages, the good that could be accomplished by such revelations, may also be used for the opposite, for so-called evil, or rather, negative manifestations of the same laws. This presents so great a danger, in terms of the laws involved, that the general good could, through ignorance, be completely annihilated.

"What good, then, is Alchemy, if it cannot be utilized for the general good? Chemistry is an open door for all mankind to enter and to benefit from." Here, truly, critics have ground on which to stand. The one and only excuse, if there is any at all in this difficult issue, must be repeated, as stated earlier: "All things are not for the *use* of everyone, although they were created for the benefit of all." If the author had to coin the above phrase, it was only with the object in mind of illustrating the cosmic wisdom, and not with the intention of excluding anyone from benefiting from alchemical knowledge. No great intellect is required to comprehend the reasoning behind our statement. Certainly no one in his right mind would feed an infant raw cabbage. Even critics will concede that those subjects belonging to psychology and representing the threshold to transcendental regions must be taken into account. The issue is all-encompassing and must not be oversimplified. That is why insufficient knowledge about such immensely important subjects only results in frustration and faulty conclusions. Such far-reaching hypotheses as the law of karma may yet serve to close the open circle that still confronts today's puzzled scientific mind.

Alchemy and Therapeutics

Students of medicine and surgery will shake their heads over efforts to connect Alchemy and therapeutics. Yet who has not stood in awe before the first corpse that revealed its marvelous anatomy to the student's searching eye? The physical organism was present—but the life force—life itself—that mystery of mysteries—had vanished. If the power of cosmic organization is so evident in the human body, why disregard the primary force that animates our total physical functioning? *Primary* force! Here is the portal to the great halls of arcane science, to the Temple of Cosmic Wisdom wherein lies the secret of creation. The Hyle of Alchemy. In what better place can one observe alchemical procedures demonstrated? Science must, of necessity, be demonstrable. It *can* be demonstrated, since it is a physical process depending upon the performer. Suppose, then, that a surgeon performs an operation. His success with one patient encourages him to repeat the same method on another and still another, only to be confronted, finally, with a failure of his procedure or operative technique on a patient who fails to respond. What of his clinical demonstration? Has he demonstrated the infallibility of his procedure? Patients may, and in fact, do respond differently to identical treatments. What makes them respond differently? Excluding abnormalities, all are endowed with the same basic organism, unless tampered with. The surgeon's success depends on the body's functioning in a normal or abnormal manner. But, we may ask in return, what determines whether a body functions normally or abnormally? I may be accused of philosophizing, but how can a physician be of help without *being* a philosopher, when normal or abnormal physical functioning produces different responses in different patients, and a multitude of philosophical and psychological factors influence what those responses will be?

Let us ask, then, "How can a physician afford to pretend to a knowledge of physical functioning, when he is ignorant of the 'thing-in-itself,' which can only be found in the realm of psychology?" He cannot afford to practice as a true son of the Hippocratic art unless he understands the invincible laws of psychology as well as he understands the techniques of wielding the scalpel or the dosage of vials of medicine. It is the combination of his understanding of the psychological as well as the physical that will result in the third point of perfection, according to the cosmic law of the triangle: the restoration of normal functioning as cosmically decreed for the individual.

It is important to note that we emphasize the *individual*. As we have pointed out in previous pages, inherent powers may be activated to various uses producing results of different proportions. Once this has become part of the consciousness of the true searcher for alchemical secrets, the path to a new and greater horizon will be opened. In the on-going search for greater knowledge and truth, the physicians of our own day are still distinctly idealistic materialists. This is exemplified by their procedures on the surgical table. The diseased *object* attracts their first attention. In most cases, they consider its removal to be a cure. But can it be? That which is no more, how can it be cured? We remove the thyroid gland of a child, and what will result? Will such a dwarfed imbecile be "cured"? We may feed the child thyroid glands orally, and growth will be resumed. But is its thyroid gland "cured"? No! The thyroid gland is missing, and this little ductless shield has not been cured, because it simply is not there any more, and the myxedema becomes evident. Gland hormones may be fed to accumulate directly in the bloodstream, but what will act internally to produce more thyroid hormones? The pituitary gland? Not likely. This endocrine is of a different consciousness. It is here that we find ourselves up against the locked portal of psychological phenomena.

What gives each gland a different consciousness, so that each produces a different hormone? Why does a cell of a different consciousness create a tumor if mislocated in the body? Does surgical skill really cure that which has been removed? Has the medical profession begun to realize its inadequacy in employing physical therapy only? If it has, then the time has arrived to delve into alchemical mysteries. Here, with honest endeavor, the medical profession may succeed in discovering undreamed-of marvels, to the praise and glory of a cosmic intelligence that reserves them for the honest, searching mind, and not merely for the servants on the Aesculapian altar. Some, among the generally honorable profession of medicine and surgery, may, like the mystified Greek god, then attempt to cut off the patient's head, bleed him, replace the cerebrum—and consider him healed!

Medical science has progressed tremendously. But has not Galen triumphed for over 1400 years only to be succeeded? Does not medical science still search within the human body to locate what, in its estimation, is superfluous, what parts are to be removed as nonessential? Yet it is nature that produces; humans can only imitate her. No substitute ever replaced an original. It may resemble but can never replace it. If then, out of an attempted imitation, a new result is produced, then it is original because it manifests in a newer, different form. So if human organs change due to natural environment, they will naturally adjust themselves. In most cases, changes are one-sided and are brought about artificially and too rapidly, thus hindering other organs in their natural, progressive adjustment. To instigate one rapid improvement in a given area will logically overtax other organs, which, due to insufficient yet accelerated power, will begin to overwork and eventually collapse, creating disorder and disease. To continue to inject stimulants under these circumstances will prove harmful and disruptive, causing the vital life force to seek more harmonious surroundings, forcing it, in extreme cases, to leave the physical body, and thus bringing about stagnation and death.

The physician's work, therefore, should be, first of all, to help to *prevent* bodily disorders and disease. Second, to help to *restore* diseased organs to normal functioning, not by removing, but by curing them. Only if he is incapable of curing them, may he remove organs, in order to prevent them from spreading disease to other areas of the body. This definitely does not permit him to use the surgical scalpel in all cases. Every time he makes use of the knife, he is taking refuge under the surgeon's emergency permission. After being permitted to practice what he learned during his college days, if the physician does not endeavor to gain more knowledge *as physician,* rather than as an expert in surgical removal of certain organs or areas of the body, he may be considered failing in his calling to serve mankind. Bearing in mind the exception noted above, his ultimate object will be to discard surgery almost entirely. Merely because this state has not been attained presently by the medical profession, need not mean that it cannot be attained in the future. We neither deny nor disparage the great skill of the medical men of today. We only urge that some among them may have the courage to go beyond their present orthodoxy, rich in accomplishment though it is, to dare to study with an open mind the works of Paracelsus and others who propounded the teachings of Alchemy. It is men such as these, both in the profession of medicine and elsewhere, who will help in the great cosmic cycle of evolution to elevate humanity and to bring the human body to its preordained state of perfection.

Alchemy and Philosophy

It was Plato's contention that *ideas* are the realization of all that matter is not. This concept has become so all-prevailing that many have forgotten the contention of his pupil, Aristotle, that ideas are *in* matter, not separated from it. Present teachings have become so confused and confusing that, for instance, in our present day tabulation of more than one hundred elements, there are, according to scientific postulations, substances which are reduced to their first nature and cannot be changed. The "infallibility" of this statement has been demonstrated by science itself in its successful smashing of certain elements into quite different ones. The ancients declared that there are only four elements that cannot be changed; namely, fire, water, air and earth. Exoteric science and professional theorists have been busy for 2,400 years working to discredit this idea and proceeding to construct intellectual Towers of Babel, which they maintained were sound and enduring.

These very structures are now beginning to collapse about their heads. The return to the road of true science, woefully neglected, must again be considered, if valid and lasting results are to be obtaned. So many "laws" in the past were accepted as irrefutable and eternal, only to be superseded by newer developments in research, as illustrated above in the successful changing of so-called "unchangeable" elements.

From the remote times of Thales to Anaxagoras (the latter is credited with the hypothesis that there must be more than four elements, causing a by-passing of *some* of Aristotle's fundamental laws), science and philosophy have followed for over two thousand years an apparently misleading theory. Before going any further, it must be admitted by the unbiased student of science and philosophy that the Atomists of ancient Greece (such men as Leucippus and Democritus) were correct. Democritus, for instance, insisted that there are many elements—it is safe to say he meant many atomic structures—in fact, that the whole universe is composed of atomic structures. We may say that it is here that our present atomic theory has its commencement, as far as man's positive search begins. Who knows of anyone changing the four elements of the ancient philosophers into different ones? An easy escape may be attempted by saying water (liquid) can be changed into hydrogen and oxygen. It cannot be changed into hydrogen and oxygen because it represents both. H_2O *is* water (liquid). One may separate and analyze it, but it cannot be changed. Therefore, it is unlikely that an element *is* what abstract science has postulated it to be. What are now termed elements are atomic components. Atoms are matterized, segmentary entities of cosmic consciousness, manifesting in one of the three elements of physical phenomena, i.e., solid, liquid or gaseous. Atomic structures can be rearranged, but the results will manifest in one of the three elements as mentioned, changes being brought about through heat (the fourth). All motion is due to force and all force emanates from heat (energy), having its origin in the universal plasma, which is a coagulation of gaseous, liquid and solid substance.

Heat, or fire, as confusingly (yet understandably) misnamed in former times, is another element. However, visible fire is combustion, a rearrangement of atomic structures, and has its origin in either solid, liquid, or gaseous combustible atomic structures. But solids (matter is a term used to describe any one of the electronic manifestations) can be liquified and liquids can become gases, and gases condensed into liquids, science will reply. True, but this is as far as it will go. An ultimate end must be reached within the realm of these elements. It can only be one of the three at one time, because all three are in one, namely heat, energy, the universal plasma. Anything that manifests to our senses does so within the three elements through the fourth. It can be only one at a time, never all three at the same instant, except in pristine form. Hydrogen and oxygen will be gases when separated; in the combination H_2O they form a liquid. Our present day misnamed elements are therefore only electronic combinations into atomic premonstrations, and these manifestations are now only approximately over 100 in number. If then any substance (erroneously called an element) represents the three actual elements that are in reality but one (the philosophical seeds, or Philosopher's Mercury), this hypothetical one must be found, for herein lies the secret of all matter, whether solid, liquid or gaseous. It cannot be common heat, because the latter represents activated force to manifest the first three. For example, a common piece of metal, say iron, may be pounded, and it will become so hot that a fire can be kindled with it. This substance (iron) represents a solid, has inherent heat (fire), can be melted into a liquid that gives off gases (air), to cool again, without activated heat, into a solid (or if burned long enough, into ferric oxide, etc.). The same may be accomplished with gases. Gas under compression may liquify or solidify. Since these constitute facts, and truth cannot be changed (knowledge can be changed), no author can take credit for it because the *idea* is incorporated in matter (substance) and of cosmic entity. There is no "origin" to it, only an entity. This entity *is* in itself, as mind is conscious entity. This conscious entity is the IDEA of Aristotle, inherent in the fifth essence or quintessence of the alchemists' four elements (they included fire as an element), to represent it in its oneness or first substance, the *prima materia.*

Now all alchemists claim that this *quintessentia* must be obtained before anything can be accomplished in Alchemy. Can it be obtained? The answer is yes. For that which exists as "idea" also exists in matter, incorporated as heat. Therefore, sensible heat exists, just as the "idea" of the *quintessentia* must be incorporated in the latter. One without the other cannot exist. It is by approaching the subject from the foregoing viewpoint that we can attempt to vindicate and to demonstrate the validity of the writings of the alchemists. Their allegorical phraseology is employed merely as a method of concealment. "Red lion," "green dragon," "dragon's blood"—these are not terms to be taken literally, any more than the Philosopher's Mercury, Sulphur and Salt are the common substances we know by those names. Experimentation based on such literal readings of the alchemists' works is bound to end in failure.

It will be evident from the foregoing that through conscientious study, a new path must be hewn for science to become worthy of man's destiny of becoming one with the absolute. Realizing that it is the inherent "idea" that is real, not the sensible manifestation, will help to make the preparatory work easier. But first of all, individuals must learn to examine more carefully the concepts presented to them, and not merely accept them blindly without inquiring into their rationality.

A new dispensation is dawning for humanity when the portals of Alchemy will be opened wider to admit the honest searcher for cosmic truth. But let it not be forgotten that even such small gates as Paracelsus and others are presently large enough to admit, one by one into the outer court of creation, those students diligent enough to search out the keys to their work.

Unfortunately, compilers and expounders have added so much of their own opinions and ideas to the writings of philosophers and alchemists that one can take, for instance, three versions by three different authors of the life of Paracelsus, only to put them down more confused than when he began. Each writer explains the life of this great sage according to his own individual interpretation. Who, then, is to be believed? If one is fortunate enough to acquire an actual unabridged copy of an alchemical author's original work, such copy, in whatever form, may safely be considered authentic. It is always best to obtain information from the original source rather than through various interpretative channels. Then, after thoughtful, intensive study of the original, the student can form his own conclusions. If the conclusions arrived at are correct, they will be found to correspond with other findings, also acquired independently, and upon these one may make further formulations, and so on, indefinitely. Just as there is no end to atomic rearrangements, so there is no end to formulating conclusions based on correct premises. Settlement of one conclusion is the beginning of a higher and more advanced hypothesis. This process is not limited to time. It is an entity in itself. Such an entity is drawing a hypothetical line only of its own entity, and time is therefore incorporated in it.

In formulating laws, it is necessary to have a norm to go by. Time, or its mathematical equivalent in numerical symbols, thanks to Pythagoras, constitutes the norm in the formulation of all man-made laws. However, cosmic laws are not themselves limited by our time and number concepts; their vibratory activity constitutes an entity superseding the Pythagorean laws of numbers. Although certain vibrations can be recorded and measured by man, making them comprehensible to him, these vibratory rates are only physical actualities, not absolute realities. For instance, if red, as science claims, vibrates at a rate of between 47,000,000,000 and 52,000,000,000 per second (or a wavelength of approximately 7,000 angstrom units), producing specific chromatic conditions in the retina, this constitutes a man-made concept of the physical actuality being described.

The postulation of seven prismatic colors, three primary and three secondary, leaves one (indigo) to be classified by itself. This classification is purely physical, as light waves can be measured and even their physical origin can be determined by spectro-analysis. Yet all seven analyzed colors are the product of a single ray of so-called white light penetrating the prism.

Now alchemists have an answer for a similar problem concerning metals by explaining that there are also seven primary metals: namely, gold, silver, copper, tin, iron, lead and mercury. Paracelsus discovered zinc, a solid metal comparable to the unstable mercury. Mercury, although a metal, is not of the same malleable nature as the first six metals. In a like manner, indigo, in the prismatic color scheme, is not one of the three primary or three secondary colors, but represents a seventh factor, separate from the others. Indigo has a bluish mixed tint, just as mercury has a silvery appearance, yet neither one is what its apparent color indicates. Indigo is not blue, nor is mercury (quicksilver) silver. If all colors can be produced from white light, then it is possible to reduce them again into white light. What indigo's place may be in this schematic arrangement has not yet been satisfactorily answered, but it is my hypothesis that it is the agent to dispel and to reorganize the different vibrations of color, similar to the role played by quicksilver among the metals. Metals are of similar origin. All seven primary metals are of one nature, just as the seven prismatic colors are drawn from a single beam of white light. If the origin of the prime metals has not been solved, it is due to the reluctance of science to accept the findings of the alchemists. Newton tried without success to win acceptance of his theory of light. Paracelsus and others also tried in vain to interest science in their findings, only to be confronted by the unseeing eye and deaf ear of prejudice.

In my careful study of the writings of the ancients, I have dared to venture beyond the familiar paths of scientific orthodoxy and conventional scholarship—yes, even traveling at times in opposite directions to see if something has not been overlooked or discarded that deserves to be recovered and more carefully examined. In the course of these studies, I have come to the realization that the Philosopher's Mercury is the source of all seven primary metals, as, in like manner, white light is the source of the seven prismatic colors. In making this statement, I am fully aware that many will scoff, and ask, "Very well, where is your Philosopher's Mercury? Show it to us and prove your theory, and we will believe you." But for the reasons cited previously, this question, for the time being, must remain unanswered.

All phenomena are threefold; there is no *physical oneness*. All physical manifestations, even those apparently single and individual in nature, have a threefold origin; otherwise, manifestation could not occur. This basic trinity is represented by the Philosophical Sulphur, Salt and Mercury, always constituting apparent oneness. Duality, negative and positive, is merely an individual concept to describe physical manifestation. From concepts such as this, based on physical phenomena, conclusions are formed. Since physical actualities are not absolute realities, but change due to constant atomic rearrangement, the conclusions formed constitute only a hypothesis based on physical experience and do not represent an absolute reality. Therefore, that which IS, exists because of its own consciousness. That which IS embraces all that we can experience consciously or subconsciously. To think of that which IS as dual is only an individual concept based on physical manifestation. A thing that IS may be interpreted as perfectly good by one person and horribly evil by another, both interpretations being applied to the same entity that IS. In reality, it cannot be both, but only one. This absolute one, or as Kant has called it, the "thing-in-itself" ("Das Ding an Sich"), constitutes consciousness of itself inherent in every cell or wherever consciousness makes itself manifest. Every duality has its origin in one cosmic consciousness. Here again it is the alchemist who diligently advocates this vital principle of the oneness of all things.

What is it that differentiates and distinguishes individual concepts? From what source do we derive our power to form concepts (if we continue in the Socratic manner to search for answers)? It is based on consciousness. To *conceive* without being conscious is impossible. We may, however, subconsciously receive and register impressions, because we are conscious of our own individuality. Man is continually confronted by a vast range of matter of varying degrees of individuality, all of it in the process of becoming apparent as it IS. All that has individuality is conscious, and all that is conscious is individual, though emanating from one source. This one source is the absolute cosmic consciousness, the only absolute reality, of which individual consciousness is a segment. This sole reality IS in itself. Because of it, the individual consciousness is *prima intelligentia,* and so it finds itself subject to a recurring law of cycles; this is not, however, the mere repetition of a common circle closing over itself again and again, but a progressive upward spiral of attainment that ultimately brings the individual into full cosmic consciousness. The step that follows is beyond our present comprehension, as the highest conceivable physical entity has not been reached as yet. When it is, another hypothetical line may be drawn, and a new set of theories formulated.

To think is to be conscious, and our terrestrial thinking occurs in time. When Aristotle explains that the distinguishing feature of man is his reason, it only means evolution from animal instinct to a higher degree of consciousness. An animal, though not "self-conscious" as we experience it, is just as aware of its own being as it is of a tree or herb. Conscious animal instinct differs from man's conscious thinking and the reasoning power it evolved, just as reasoning ability itself is undeveloped in comparison to cosmic consciousness. Cosmic consciousness does not have to reason, for it is the source of all that IS. It is the highest conceivable norm by which man can reason. Extensive conscious reasoning must eventually arrive at a hypothetical dividing line of its own entity awareness. In some cases this has been accomplished. The hypothetical line has thereupon been drawn, and the new entity of cosmic consciousness based upon it.

Attaining the summit of alchemical knowledge, wherein cosmic consciousness is experienced as subject and the *quintessentia* as object, has climaxed the noble quest of sages since time immemorial. It represents man's zenith, his mastership over matter and the eventual merging into one with the Absolute, the realization of cosmic consciousness.

APPENDIX

To encourage neophytes in their noble alchemical quest for the attempted procurement of the Philosopher's Stone, it may not be amiss to mention a few of the varied experiences of the writer in his many years of mental, spiritual and practical research.

Not everyone will have the good fortune to have access to the numerous books published on Alchemy, as many of them have become exceedingly rare and difficult to obtain. Most of these works are now out of print, and those who own and treasure them are not likely to part with them. Consequently, high prices are being asked by many booksellers for these rare editions. However, we cannot overestimate the true value of certain of these works, such as *The Hermetical and Alchemical Writings of Paracelsus* in two volumes, edited by A. E. Waite; Basil Valentine's *Triumphant Chariot of Antimony; Collectanea Chemica; Turba Philosophorum; The New Pearl of Great Price* by Bonus of Ferrara, and other works that will prove of great value to the student. The writings of Franz Hartmann also deserve mention for those students who can fathom the thought-world permeating his books. Another monumental publication is the famous *Secret Symbols of the Rosicrucians of the Sixteenth and Seventeenth Centuries (Geheime Figuren der Rosenkreuzer, aus dem 16ten und 17ten Jahrhundert,* Altona, Germany, 1785-88, 2 vols.). Dr. Franz Hartmann brought one copy of this extremely rare work to America and had it partly translated into English. (Dr. Hartmann's published version omits about a third of the original plates and part of the German text). It was the writer's good fortune to obtain a copy of the complete work. It made necessary a trip to Europe, where his amanuensis, at the same time, obtained another copy also. It is remarkable how the Divine Will operates to open ways and provide means for the sincere searcher to obtain some of the arcane wisdom as well as the equipment requisite to his work. Of the lamentably few con-

117

temporary works on Alchemy, we would cite *Alchemy Rediscovered and Restored* by Archibald Cockren. In spite of the obvious omission of certain phrases, this work will prove valuable in providing answers to the problems involved.

Although we cannot mention in detail the numerous successes it has been our good fortune to achieve in the laboratory, many landmarks stand out in our memory: when, after a long and wearisome process, the essence of gold was first extracted; when the vinegar of antimony was likewise produced from the *Spiessglas* glass of antimony), according to the formula of Valentine, and a red tincture produced. When we recall these experiences, it does not matter any more what sceptics say, or that scoffers deride the claims of Valentine that this balm of antimony would cure leprosy and ulcers that have been alive with worms or cancer. Theodore Kerckringius, Valentine's commentator and himself a physician, demonstrated the truth of Valentine's assertions when other surgeons requested the amputation of a patient's breast that was twice the size of the other and filled with cancerous matter.

How well we recall the scene when, more than twenty-five years ago, we first obtained the essence (or oil, as we prefer to call it) of copper. It was such a small quantity. But how grateful we felt after proving before our own eyes what previous studies had indicated was possible. The test tube containing it is still in our possession and stands as an encouraging testimony when failure in experimentations with different substances occasionally occurs. Likewise, the oil of lead was extracted. What a glorious moment it was, when unwavering faith was finally substantiated.

Now when I open the incubator door, look through the inner glass door, and see the Erlenmeyer flasks standing there with the essence of gold exhibiting a rich golden color where before only a nonacetous menstruum, clear and pure as water, showed no color at all; or where the herbal extracts in their high potency, mingle with their own purified salts, nestling among other flasks in the gentle warmth, beside containers of equal or greater importance—what do I care then for those who ridicule Alchemy? The time will come, and it is not far off, as the masters of our art have stated, when more and more of our secret art will be made known to worthy searchers. More and more people are leaving the narrow confines of their religious creeds, not to denounce them—O, no!—but thankful that they have helped them to receive the greater light, always remembering gratefully the wonderful instructions they have received, which made it possible to venture into the great seeming void that begins now to take shape in recognizable dimensions.

Those searching souls, likewise, will have similar experiences. They, too, will find the truth hidden behind the simplest principles and laws of nature. For nature is the outward expression of God.

Whatever the cost in time, labor or money, rest assured it will prove itself worth your while; and if you should be unable to procure the Philosopher's Stone in this life, remember that you have laid the foundation for another, better one, in which you will be enabled to attain your goal, after serving your apprenticeship. And yet, who knows but that the Divine Will, through its karmic wisdom, may grant you the ability to obtain this priceless gem.

My work is not to revolutionize the scientific world. As a humble servant for a greater one yet to come, who, as in former times, had a great work to perform and will do so again— in his service do I find happiness and contentment. To have been found worthy to be initiated into such profound wisdom alone constitutes a great blessing.

With the Hermetic Masters, since time immemorial, through the Middle Ages and up to the present day, I can acclaim, NOT in a vain religious way, but devoutly and piously, from the bottom of a grateful heart:

God be praised, for He is *so good* to us, children.

ALCHEMICAL MANIFESTO

1960

Because the term Alchemy is associated by most people solely with the Philosopher's Stone and the making of gold, it is essential that this false notion be corrected. Alchemy, as such, covers an enormous area and is concerned primarily with the raising of vibrations. Its varied and many-sided manifestations are the outcome of profound study and contemplation. Since only a few, among the billions of people inhabiting this globe, are actively engaged in the alchemical work, it is vitally important that we concern ourselves with a correct approach to this subject.

The immense scope of alchemystical investigations makes it difficult to understand why so few are actively engaged in this work, for its manifestations are of such tremendous importance they transcend the common belief of the casual observer.

In former ages, Alchemists concealed themselves in damp cellars and sweltering garrets. Their hideaways were hard to detect. Likewise, their mode of communication with brother and sister adepts was confined to a symbolic and hidden nature. All this and many other difficulties and restrictions were imposed by the circumstances prevailing in previous historical periods.

Even in this new cycle of alchemystical awakening, there still exists a certain necessity to commence our work cautiously. In spite of freedoms not enjoyed in former times, we must exercise a due degree of care as we proceed to make contact with those of like mind and similar aspirations—aspirations that may have lain dormant for many years, and interests that, in fact, antedate their present incarnation.

To forestall any misunderstanding, it is hoped that the following paragraphs will help to make our position clear. In them we will try to answer the most frequently asked questions:

Why do the Alchemists of the Paracelsus Research Society give no street address, only a post office box number?

Why are the names of those representing or governing the society not given out to the public?

Why are there no memberships?

Why are the Bulletins received by individuals who, in terms of laboratory work, have hardly done anything of an alchemical nature?
We may answer the above question as follows:

The present quarters of the Paracelsus Research Society are moderate, and, just as in former times, not designed for the purpose of making itself known to the general public. The reasons for this are as valid today as they were in ages gone by. As we stated clearly in the first Bulletin issued in this dispensation, no publicity is desired. To seek it would do no good, and in the long run, would only result in the misrepresentation of the Society.

As stated also in the same Bulletin, no names of present-day contributors will be published or made known. This announcement was based on the age-old tradition that all those actively engaged in the Hermetic work do not do so in search of fame.

Since no Alchemist covets praise and glory, it should not be hard to understand that there is no need for personal acknowledgment. Furthermore, it could lead, with some, to a personality cult, and this is entirely irrelevant. The work itself is the important thing, never personalities.

There is no necessity for individuals to become affiliated members who pay dues or become confined within the sort of restrictions one necessarily finds in any organized group or society. Alchemical aspirants should be free—free in their thinking and free in their actions.

There is a right time and place for the obligations of group activity and group discipline, and many who are emerging into awareness of the alchemystical work are already members of fraternal organizations designed for that specific type of activity. These persons will find themselves becoming better and more devout members of their respective fraternal affiliations, deriving from them a greater understanding of the beauty and value of rightly performed rituals.

Some have suggested that Alchemists should group themselves into colonies and devote their time and efforts exclusively to the pursuit of alchemical work, unmolested by outsiders. However sincere such a suggestion may be, it is entirely inconsistent with the work to be performed by the Paracelsus Research Society. Those urging restricted alchemical "communes" are not far enough advanced to realize that nothing would be gained by such a procedure. Our work is here, among mankind. Amidst the hustle and bustle of everyday life is the place for us to overcome the shortcomings still adhering to us as humans. The time for the individual's personal isolation from society will come only after a prolonged—and successful—period of preliminary work. Only then will he receive higher instructions in order to perform a specific work. But this is not the case with the average student of Alchemy, and only rarely with the advanced ones. True, advanced students of the Hermetic work will be given an opportunity to conceal themselves for a period of seven weeks at the utmost, in a retreat in a high mountainous place here in the western part of the United States. But that will be the case only in limited instances and only after thorough and proper preparation. After this period of study and meditation, even these advanced aspirants will return to the ways of everyday life to apply what they have learned in their daily lives. When such individuals are chosen, it will be solely upon their merits and absolutely free of any fee, cost or remittance of a pecuniary nature. Since there will never be more than twelve aspirants together at one time, one can well imagine how limited such opportunities are. No restriction, however, will be placed on the individual's social, racial, religious, fraternal, financial or educational standing. The spiritual development will be the decisive factor. This statement should suffice to make it quite clear that anyone who meets the requirements is eligible for consideration.

Bulletins have been received by individuals who have never done any alchemical laboratory work. Some, perhaps, are only vaguely acquainted with the subject. The reason is that either a previous contact with the work had been established, or the individual concerned may contact another person, who is ready to commence the work. Contacts are made at times in rather strange ways. Only later, after considerable time has elapsed, will the purpose of such contacts become fully understood.

Anyone suspecting this work of being a commercialized enterprise, utilized for the personal gain or profit of any individual connected with its administration, is, in the first place, not qualified merely by harboring such thoughts, and, secondly, he has only to engage in some simple arithmetic to allay his suspicions. It will be apparent to anyone familiar with today's astronomically high printing, mailing and correspondence costs, that our modest subscription fee can scarcely be said to cover even these expenses.

But we were not intended to be a commercially rewarding enterprise. The ways and means to accomplish the work set forth for the Paracelsus Research Society will be available as they are needed. The resources will be found, and more cannot be said. Since this work is of an unselfish nature, it will be evident that our Bulletins, limited to a printing of 500 copies, have sometimes been sent out to subscribers who have not responded; that in some cases, no significant contact is made. But there is no rush about this. Some of our Bulletins, not fully subscribed, are being held back for others with whom contact will be made later. Our *Alchemical Laboratory Bulletins,* though numbered, are timeless. A hundred years from now, they will be as applicable as they are today.

Anyone reading this Manifesto is hereby invited to give this matter serious consideration. Not everything that greets our senses is met with full understanding on first contact. Psychologists have likened our conscious mind to that visible portion of an iceberg that represents only a fraction of its actual dimensions. For some of us, making contact with the Paracelsus Research Society is like viewing that iceberg. Meditation will open up what has been, and for some still is, concealed from our understanding. This is the key that will open the portal to the new world of the Alchemists, a world that you are already aware of and acquainted with, through karma, through previous incarnations, or whatever terms may be applied.

May the Cosmic Light guide and direct you in your sincere endeavors, and may you be one of those to glorify the works of the Divine by becoming an administrator of the heavenly bounties among mankind.

Surely it is better to be one of those actively engaged in the Hermetic work, leaving for posterity a record of accomplishment, than to remain an outsider who only *reads* about others and what they have been able to perform.

May a deep and abiding PEACE permeate your whole being, and may you be engulfed in the radiations from the endless Love of the God of your Heart.

Given at the sixth day in May, A.D. 1960.